Kitchen Utensils

Kitchen Utensils

Names, Originals, and Definitions from the Early Middle Ages to the Mid-Nineteenth Century

Phillips V. Brooks

Graphic line illustrations by Niina Aalto, illustrator, Helsinki, Finland. All rights reserved.

All "author photos" taken at Seurasaari Open-Air Museum, Seurasaari, Helsinki, Finland. All rights reserved.

All other photographs by permission of the Collection of the Mercer Museum of the Bucks County Historical Society.

Definitions, unless noted otherwise, from Oxford English Dictionary Online, reproduced by permission of Oxford University Press.

First published 2004 by
PALGRAVE MACMILLAN™
175 Fifth Avenue, New York, N.Y. 10010 and
Houndmills, Basingstoke, Hampshire, England RG21 6XS
Companies and representatives throughout the world.

PALGRAVE MACMILLAN is the global academic imprint of
the Palgrave Macmillan division of St. Martin's Press, LLC and of
Palgrave Macmillan Ltd. Macmillan® is a registered trademark
in the United States, United Kingdom and other countries.
Palgrave is a registered trademark in the European Union
and other countries.

ISBN 1–4039–6619–2 hardback

Library of Congress Cataloging-in-Publication Data
Brooks, Phillips V.
    Kitchen Utensils: names, origins, definitions through the ages / Phillips V. Brooks.
        p. cm.
    Includes bibliographical references.
    ISBN 1–4039–6619–2 (hc: alk. paper)
        1. Kitchen utensils. I. Title

TX656.B786 2004
643'.3—dc22   2004044505

A catalogue record for this book is available from the British Library.

Design by Newgen Imaging Systems (P) Ltd., Chennai, India.

First edition: October 2004
10 9 8 7 6 5 4 3 2 1

Printed in the United States of America.

For Karen

The first foundation of a good House must be the Kitchen.

—Richard Surflet, *Estienne (c.) and Liebault's (J.)*
Maison rustique, or the *countrie farme*.
Trans. 1600. Augmented by G. Markham 1616.

Contents

Abbreviations Used in Utensils Table

Abbreviations used in the "Probable Source of Term" column and frequency of source.

AF.	Anglo-French	10
AIr.	Anglo-Irish	1
AL.*	Anglo-Latin	1
Arab.	Arabic	1
Da.	Danish	31
Du.	Dutch	46
EFris.	East Frisian	3
EGmc.*	East Germanic	1
EME.*	Early Middle English	1
Eng.	English	4
Flem.*	Flemish	11
Fr.	French	21
Gael.	Gaelic	5
Ger.	German	24
Goth.	Gothic	4
Gr.*	Greek	1
HG.*	High German	1
Hind.	Hindustani	1
Icel.	Icelandic	3
Ir.	Irish	3
It.	Italian	11

Abbreviations Used in Utensils Table

LG.	Low German	27
Loc.	Localism	1
LOE.*	Late Old English	2
LON.*	Late Old Norse	1
LSc.	Lowland Scots	1
MDu.	Middle Dutch	48
ME.	Middle English	33
Med. L.	Medieval Latin	2
MFlem.*	Middle Flemish	2
MG.*	Middle German	3
MHG.	Middle High German	43
MLG.	Middle Low German	32
MSw.*	Middle Swedish	4
NEng.*	Northern English	1
NFris.	North Frisian	4
Norw.	Norwegian	6
ODu.*	Old Dutch	2
OE.	Old English	58
OF.	Old French	72
OFris.	Old Frisian	14
OIr.	Old Irish	2
OHG.	Old High German	41
OLG.	Old Low German	6
ON.	Old Norse	39
ONF.	Old Northern Fr.	4
ONorw.	Old Norwegian	1
OSc.	Old Scotch	1
OSw.	Old Swedish	5
OTeut.	Old Teutonic	12
Pg.	Portuguese	10
Pr.	Provencal	3
Sc.	Scottish	7

Abbreviations Used in Utensils Table

Sp.	Spanish	14
Sw.	Swedish	24
W.	Welsh	1
WFlem.	West Flemish	2
WFris.	West Frisian	5
WGmc.	West Germanic	4

Source: Unless otherwise indicated by * all abbreviations from the *OED*.

Abbreviations and frequency in the "Usage" column:

Appl.	Applied	1
Arch.	Archaic	12
Dial.	Dialect	31
Hist.	Historical	4
Lit.	Literary	1
Loc.*	Local	2
N. Amer.	North America	12
N. Dial.	Northern Dialect	1
Obs.	Obsolete	68
Spec.	Specific usage	2

Acknowledgments

I would like to thank Matti Rissanen, professor emeritus, former chair of the Department of English, University of Helsinki, and currently team leader at the Research Unit for Variation and Change in English, Department of English, University of Helsinki, Finland, who provided very helpful suggestions concerning the development of the English language, as well as Rod McConchie, lecturer, Department of English, University of Helsinki, for his careful reading and supportive comments on the text. Many thanks to Jackie Schneider, reference librarian, Davis & Elkins College, Elkins, West Virginia, whose help in locating material greatly facilitated my efforts. A special thanks to Mikko Laaksonen for his very patient and professional help formatting the manuscript.

Preface

What began as an idle curiosity regarding the names and origins of kitchen utensils evolved into a search of the history of the English language as to the origin of the name for a specific utensil. The English cook in the Middle Ages had only a limited number of tools at hand and worked in a kitchen that often threatened his or her life.

Today the utensils have changed, some are no longer in use, while others have been altered in material and modified in design. Of the 383 identified utensils I found from various sources and especially in the Old English Dictionary (*OED*) there remain today in the English language over 300 kitchen utensils that still retain the same name, function, and approximately the same spelling as their original designation. I hope that this glossary will aid current and future writers as well as those with an interest about the origins, functions, and terms historically employed for kitchen utensils.

Introduction

The word "kitchen" comes down through the centuries from the Old English word "cycene," which entered England from the Germanic languages and earlier from the Latin and eventually appeared in as many as 47 variant spellings. The first recorded written use of the word occurred about the year 1000 but the word was probably widely used long prior to this date. The *Oxford English Dictionary (OED)* defines the word as "that room or part of the house in which food is cooked; a place fitted with the apparatus for cooking."

In colonial America various names were used to refer to the kitchen. It was called the "fire room" in seventeenth-century Rhode Island. In Connecticut and Massachusetts it was referred to as the "hall." The term "keeping room" was applied to the kitchen in a lean-to, a shed-like addition to the main house. When ells, a long, low shed attached to the main house, were added to the main dwelling, the names Great Kitchen, Little Kitchen, and Summer Kitchen were used.[1]

Later the word "kitchen" embraced the utensils used in the preparation of food. However, the word still retained wide use as a place and "kitchen" became an adjective modifying the word "utensils." Whether a kitchen is thought of as a fire built against a wall or stone, a fireplace within a building, or even as a fire built outdoors, it was the place where man prepared his food and made it more palatable. In the cooking of food, tools or utensils, simple and complex, were developed to assist the cook. From a very crude spit made of small branches to the elaborate andirons and later the gas or electric range, man sought or invented the required tools to ease the preparation of his meals. These tools, or utensils as they became known, were shaped by necessity to suit particular cooking tasks. Some were very simple, others more elaborate.

Antiquarians, collectors, and museums have sought out these cooking implements. Today, in the many books on the topic of kitchen utensils, filled with numerous illustrations and photographs, one can begin to see the evolution of these utensils. They all had names that were borrowed from other languages or that were invented to reflect the task intended.

It is the purpose of this inventory or glossary to list the utensils by category as far as is known at the present time. No list can ever be definitive but by careful research of articles, books, wills, and inventories a fairly comprehensive compilation has been achieved. All the words listed (see exceptions below) have been recorded from definitions in the *Oxford English Dictionary* (1st, 2nd, 3rd editions). Any variations or changes to the *Oxford* definition are indicated with square brackets.

The first column lists the word for an item as used in English, the second column indicates the variant spellings that the word exhibits, and the third column provides a definition of the word. Usage is indicated when known and the probable etymology is listed. The date indicates the first-known written use of the word. Where no information is listed in a column such information is currently unknown. To understand the reason why some of the terms underwent change, it would help to briefly trace some of the influences on the English language. Influences such as war, migration, and dominant language altered the names of utensils.

Definition of a Kitchen Utensil

The accepted definition of a kitchen is a place where food is prepared and the equipment used in the cooking of food or utensils is stored. This definition is limited, since the fireplace can hardly be considered separate from the crane or the pot. The implied definition of a utensil is its transportability, whereas the fireplace is a permanent fixture of the place defining a kitchen. For 1,000 years or more the fireplace was where the cook began and ended the cooking chores. The slow introduction of improvements to the fireplace has been generally in the form of utensils. For example, the lugpole, crane, sway, or oven are fixed attachments to the fireplace and thus not separate from the opening, yet they can be considered a utensil. The pawn might be considered an aesthetic element of the kitchen yet it is a utensil in that it helped the cook to control the draft of the fireplace.

The tools the user employed aided in the task of cooking. However, many utensils were not directly involved in food preparation. For example, the piggin, the rush light, and the trencher can be viewed as adjuncts to the kitchen, but not involved in the cooking process itself. For terms of convenience, histories of the early kitchen collectively classify all such equipment used in the kitchen as utensils. In more recent times a distinction has been made between kitchen utensils and kitchen appliances. The refrigerator, the hood vent over the stove, the disposal unit under the sink, and even the stove are generally identified as appliances as opposed to the paring knife, peeler, can opener, or the various pots and other utensils with which the modern kitchen is equipped.

Dating of Kitchen Utensils

Dating a kitchen utensil from the Middle Ages to the mid-nineteenth century is problematic. Archaeologists, museum curators, and experts in the field rely on many factors when dating an item. Knowledge of metallurgical development and processes, changes in the production of earthenware and chinaware, design and patterns, social history, and more specialized details help date an item. With iron objects or chinaware often a mark or initial on the bottom, side, or underside of a handle can be traced to a particular provenance and time. In England and Colonial America many iron utensils were hand-forged by a local smithy, employing his own creativity when making the object, but he often left no identifying mark. Often the design of an item can be placed in a particular locale as the design may be indigenous, but this method is always open to question as

an individual could have easily seen a particular design in one place, copied it, and produced the item in a different place.

With wooden items dating can generally be placed no more accurately than early, middle, or late century as seldom were such items marked by the maker with a name or place. Many wooden items became hand carved or hand turned by the user for personal use. Since such items often cracked, broke, or became no longer usable they were discarded and a new utensil was carved. However, elements of design and type of wood can be used to indicate a rough date and provenance.

Other tools used in the dating of objects are newspapers, advertisements, broadsides, references in books, diaries, letters, wills, inventories, shipping bills, ships' cargo logs, and even paintings of the period. The *OED* is useful as it indicates the earliest mention of an item in writing. Another method used in dating is by comparison if two or more similar items are under study. In the eighteenth century records of a utensil's manufacturer may have survived, thus affording a fairly accurate date. However, such information is not always absolute, since the manufacturer may have merely produced an item already widely used some place else.

Caution is the byword in such attempts at classification. Forgeries made to meet the demands of collectors or museums to complete a collection often are discovered by alert experts. Some found objects have defied identification, such as a specific tool made to prepare an ethnic meal. An example of such a utensil would be a tool for removing seeds from squash in preparation for stuffing it. Dating and identification is a problem that confronts a curator or collector after securing or receiving an item. Careful study of other known objects is required, especially if an item has more than one part. Settlers moving into the interior of America often fashioned items to use in a particular way or for a particular purpose and they were discarded when no longer needed.

A very useful volume in understanding the problems of dating is Ivor Noel Hume's *A Guide to Artifacts of Colonial America*. Although much of the book gives attention to objects unearthed at Williamsburg, Virginia, he provides interesting examples of the processes involved in accurate dating. Patience, constant study, and alertness to small clues, often seemingly unrelated, can provide a means of discovering definite dates and the origins of an item.

Coming to the New World

The *Mayflower* sailed from England in 1620. Queen Elizabeth had died 17 years earlier and William Shakespeare had been dead a scant four years. John Donne would die in 1631 and Ben Jonson would die seven years later. It was the age of the Renaissance, an intellectual and cultural movement begun in the late fifteenth century that reached its peak during the settling of America. It was an age of brilliant men—essayists, poets, dramatists, and musicians. Explorations to new lands, flourishing trade, and wars with France and Spain made for a bubbling ferment of new ideas and opportunities in London. It was also an age of discontent for those who sought religious and political freedom and especially an escape from the enclosure movement in the British Isles. Thus began an exodus of the English, the Irish, the Scots, alone and with their families, which in the late eighteenth century forced England to pass laws forbidding emigration to America. But onward they came, braving whatever hardships they would encounter.

They came in large numbers and they came if not with all their worldly goods at least with the knowledge of how tools and kitchen utensils were made and used. Once landed, whether in New England, the Middle Colonies, or the Southern Colonies, they proceeded to replicate their former home. Finding climate, soil, and space different, they soon adapted to a new way of living.

The Germanic invasions of England consisting of Jutes, Saxons, and Angles from about 410 to 420 profoundly influenced the English language. The invasions helped to establish the basis of a common spoken language for the peasantry and the then emerging aristocracy that had been in existence for over 1,500 years. The commingling of the dialects of the different invading tribes eventually merged into a single language. Old English (–1150), Middle English (1150–1500), and modern English (1500–present) all reflect the shifts in spoken and written English. Words were borrowed from other languages, notably from the Celtic, Latin, French, and Old Norse. As invaders settled into eventual peaceable harmony over two centuries they had an extensive influence in place-names and everyday communications in England.

After 1066 (Battle of Hastings) England experienced the use of two languages; English and French. The common folk continued to use Old and Middle English, the language they had known. The aristocracy, the court, churchmen, and merchants in the London environs spoke and wrote French after the Norman Conquest for over 200 years. One consequence of this bilingualism was a large body of literature in French written in England that in time introduced new words into daily life.

By the fifteenth century French slowly began to disappear. After Normandy was lost to the English crown in 1204 England began to move solidly toward the nation-state it would become.

At the onset of the fourteenth century, English was once more known by everyone, although French was used by the educated classes that included people involved in the legal profession, the church, and those merchants involved in trade with France. By 1385 English became the language taught in the schools. And by 1450 the guilds and towns were writing their books and ordinances in English. At the close of the Middle English period (1500) the English language underwent momentous changes; changes in grammar reduced English from a highly inflected language to an analytic one. In terms of vocabulary the loss of a large part of Old English word stock and the addition of thousands of words from French and Latin significantly altered the language. Thus words of Romance origin were slowly assimilated into the native English tongue.

Within England, English differed with noticeable variations in separate areas. Four principal dialects emerged; Northern, East Midland, West Midland, and Southern. It was from the East Midland and Southern areas that the early emigrants to the New World first came. The Southern dialect became the basis of Standard English as London was the capital, the center of the court, and the trading center of the country.

London English was further established as the standard in writing because of the introduction of the printing press in 1476. William Caxton (1422–1491), the first English printer, used the current speech of London in his books and translations. In spelling, pronunciation, and grammar the public absorbed Standard English through books, broadsides, published sermons, and court documents. Pronunciation in the London area slowly became uniform.

By the beginning of the sixteenth century, although English was now the mother tongue of England, wide differences remained in pronunciation and especially in spelling. Orthography was still far from uniform. Other factors influenced the English language. The expansion of the empire as well as increased trade with Europe and the Middle and Far East brought new words into the language. But in the main, the English language became fixed in approximately its present form during the sixteenth and seventeenth centuries.

The early explorers and settlers in the New World were not uneducated as evidenced from the records that have survived. Many of the passengers on the *Mayflower* were writers and well read. Thus the English language spoken in America was much the same as in England. Even after early immigrants from Germany, Holland, Ireland, Sweden, and Scotland arrived, all bringing their own languages with them, they soon began to speak English as the English settlers were the dominant population. Conventions of English spellings derived from what the writer sensed was the correct form. Earlier forms of spelling were often retained. Educational level and temperament did little to achieve consistency. Printers, in order to justify a line, often added optional letters and often imposed their own dialect. By 1550 in London some efforts were begun to draw up rules of grammar and spelling and devise new systems of spelling and grammar. In 1568 publisher Thomas Smith (1513–1579) distributed a *Dialogue Concerning the Correct and Emended Writing of the English Language*. His work was followed by other proposals in 1570 and 1580, and in 1582 Richard Mulcaster (1531?–1611), first Master of Merchant Taylor's School, London, offered the public his *Elementari*, which was devoted to English spelling. Mulcaster did not believe that spellings could ever perfectly and phonetically represent sound. Custom and usage provided the basis of his reform as well as common sense. He laid down some rules for a uniform spelling.

By 1650 modern spelling was well established. Writers such as Sir Thomas Elyot, Sir Thomas Chaloner, Roger Ascham, and Thomas Wilson all championed regularizing spelling during the Renaissance. In order to spread the acceptable spelling of words, dictionaries were produced. Robert Cawdrey (c1538) rector and schoolmaster in Oakham, Rutland County, England, wrote *A Table Alphabeticall of Hard Words* (1604) that consisted of 120 pages listing some 3,000 words. Later, in 1616, John Bullokar (1580–1641), an English lexicographer, published *English Expositor* and in 1623 Henry Cockeram, an expositer, authored and produced the first English dictionary, the *English Dictionarie*. Others followed. By no means did such compendiums attempt to include all the words in the English language. In 1721 Nathaniel Bailey (–1742), a British lexicographer, published his *Universal Etymological Dictionarie* that attempted to list all the words in the language. The basis of spelling became fixed during this period.

In the eighteenth century American reformers of spelling proposed various schemes, generally based on the most logical and rational method. Notably, in 1768, Benjamin Franklin (1706–1790), an American statesman, scientist, inventor, printer, and philosopher, while living in London, wrote *A Scheme for a New Alpabet and a Reformed Mode of Spelling*. Later, in 1793, William Thornton (1759–1828), an American architect and designer, proposed a full scheme of reforms. In 1798 and 1808 there were attempts to record the language phonetically. A stronger effort had been submitted to Congress in 1786 by Noah Webster, textbook author, spelling reformer, and lexicographer, in a campaign for nationalizing the English language in America. His plan was not acted upon. Webster's impact on spelling is notable in his *A Grammatical Institute of the American Language* (1783), better known as *The American Spelling Book* (1787), which by 1829 was known as *The Elementary Spelling Book* or the "Blue-backed Speller" because of its blue cover. Webster's work is partly based on English schoolmaster Thomas Dilworth's *Guide to the English Tongue*, a work widely reprinted in America. Webster's book underwent considerable revisions in its many subsequent editions with spelling alterations

based on the authority of "approved authors of the last and present century."[1] The *American Spelling Book* was widely adopted by schools, so much so that by 1818 over five million copies were sold. Webster's name is firmly entrenched in American culture as the maker of dictionaries. His first dictionary was published in 1806. This was followed in a shorter form in 1807 in which he claimed to contain "all the words which common people have occasion to use."[2] Webster's spellings are simplifications omitting silent letters, dropping the final double consonants, and deleting the final silent "e" when not needed. Eventually the differences between American and English spellings were brought into closer accord.

That Webster and others who tried to reform spelling often failed to find acceptance was the result of the reluctance of the public to deviate from tradition and custom. Thus dictionaries came to reflect common usage by speakers and writers rather than being the final arbiters of the language.

In the eighteenth century the appeal to authority for a sense of order and the value of regulation prevailed in both England and America. The age wanted to "fix" the language. Samuel Johnson (1709–1784), a famous English lexicographer, produced his *Dictionary* in 1755. In spite of many faults it reflected the accepted spelling and origin of words, thus making it a great contribution to the record of usage. Since its publication philologists have further refined the etymologies and engaged in a systematic and scientific study of the English language.

The large influx of German, Dutch, Scots-Irish, Scots, the Irish, and, later, groups of immigrants from Middle Europe have had an impact on language in America.

Although immigrants settled in America from many lands, the majority of immigrants were English and the dominant tongue prevailed. The English were in positions of power as to what language would be taught in the schools, which had quite a standardizing influence. English was also the language used in the courts and the political life of the times. In the 150 years prior to 1776 non-English immigrants tended to assimilate the major language in use. Cultural and linguistic assimilation is a slow and conservative process, but over time, each immigrant population adopted English. Jeremy Smith, an English language scholar, very ably traces not only the history and evolution of the English language but lucidly explains linguistic evolution, the intra- and extralinguistic change within a society and scribal translations. To generalize, in the infusion of the many languages entering North America from 1620 to 1850 three stages of linguistic change are evident. According to Smith language change occurs when there is "the potential for change, the triggering and implementation of change, [and] the diffusion of change."[3] One can conjecture that the terminology for kitchen utensils changed accordingly. Some terms fell out of use while new terms were accepted at the same time supporting the "principle of maintaining intelligibility."[4] Each succeeding generation would speak the dominant language.

Albert C[roll]. Baugh, an American literary scholar and linguist, and

Thomas Cable address the issue of linguistic change, claiming that Americans achieved uniformity in their usage of English because of the high mobility of the people. There was constant "mingling of the settlers from one part with settlers from other parts."[5] They state, that "as each new section [of the country] was opened up it attracted colonists from various districts which had become over-crowded or uncongenial to them."[6] It should also be recognized that many new and older immigrants were seeking land on the edges of already claimed land, thus going further afield and intermixing with others. Consequently the English language in America acquired a high degree of uniformity in spite of regional differences.

Baugh quotes Isaac Candler, an Englishman who traveled in America from 1822 to 1823. Candler wrote, "The United States having been peopled from different parts of England and Ireland, the peculiarities of the various districts have in a great measure ceased."[7] Complete linguistic uniformity cannot be a claim as there remained regional pockets where non-English speech prevailed until well into the nineteenth century and beyond. The Pennsylvania Dutch, Germans, and Swiss clung to their native language as did the Swedes, Finns, and Norwegians who settled in Minnesota and the Midwest. The concentration of a native language in a regional area is characterized by linguists as "variational space." The English language did rule, although in rural America it ruled more conservatively than it did along the Atlantic coast and in the major cities.

The growth of trades and manufacture in the colonies that improved existing utensils made some earlier tools obsolete. Further, England, having found the colonies a ready market for their products, introduced new utensils developed in Europe. Yankee ingenuity, resourcefulness, and the sheer need to make the kitchen safer and the preparation of food easier certainly prompted many of the earlier utensils to fall into disuse. The introduction of the crane, the side oven, the English Dutch oven, cresset dogs, and pot sways made the work of the cook considerably safer and improved the quality of food. Hearth death was second only to childbirth as the most common cause of death for women during the Elizabethan period and later in the colonies.

Necessity was the mother of invention for the frontier settler who needed utensils not otherwise available. Carved from wood or shaped from scrap metal the utensils were utilitarian and served immediate needs. Because of the constraints of frontier travel and the burden of excess weight, settlers would take only those utensils that were absolutely necessary when they left populous eastern regions to settle further west. An iron pot could serve many purposes, and one might suffice on the frontier where an array of pots had been on hand previously. However, iron pots are easily broken or cracked so care was exercised in transporting these and other valuable tools into the interior of the country. Ladles, spoons, flesh forks, trenchers, and bowls only needed the settlers' time to be carved from the abundance of wood.

Utensils that served identical purposes were called different names in various regions. The general trend toward uniformity in language usage in America worked also to standardize the naming of kitchen utensils. However, many of the regional appellations have survived to the present time. For example, in New England the word "spider" is often given to a frying pan that is known as a "skillet" in the South. Another example is the word for a paper bag: in New England and other areas it is called a "bag" or "sack" but in many areas of Kentucky, Tennessee, West Virginia, and the South it is called a "poke." As late as 1970 I purchased a small amount of groceries in Letterbox, Kentucky, and was asked by the clerk if I wanted a poke. Needless to say I was confused as this was my first encounter with the word in this sense.

Linguistic atlases such as *The Linguistic Atlas of the United States and Canada*, which began in 1929, resulted in 12 regional atlases providing ample evidence of the levels of usage and geographic range of terms in America. Also helpful is Peter M. Anderson's *A Structural Atlas of the English Dialects*.

Some of the earliest settlers in America were separatists from the Church of England known as Pilgrims. There appears to be no record of the kitchen utensils brought by the Pilgrims on their voyage in the *Mayflower* in 1620. Prior to its departure from England, Christopher Martin was engaged to secure provisions for the ship's crew and passengers, but no record survives. However, a listing of wills and inventories of household possessions in colonial America by Richard B. Bailey reveals that articles such as trenchers, cups, bowls, leather and pewter bottles, beakers, pewter platters and plates, salts, andirons, frying pans, porringers, iron and brass kettles, ladles, mortar and pestles, pothooks and pot hangers, slices, skillets, sieves, and trammels were fairly common in the early 1620s.[8] Such utensils were all common in England at the time. Cooking on the voyage was done on the open deck. After landing at Cape Cod and finally settling at Plymouth fires were built and food prepared. The history of the Pilgrims has been well recorded and documented. Their

sufferings in the first year are part of the lore of the founding of the New World in 1620. In their explorations, according to Mourt's *Relations* (regarded as a collaboration by William Bradford and Edward Winslow), they picked up a big iron kettle used by the Indians, obviously a ship's kettle "brought out from Europe"[9] probably by some English or Breton fishermen who occasionally visited the coast previously. The Pilgrims tried to carry the kettle filled with maize back to the *Mayflower* but abandoned it because of its weight. Further explorations in the area revealed Indian huts from which the Pilgrims took away many wooden trays and dishes, earthen pots, and an English bucket without a handle.

From the records remaining it is evident the Pilgrims had the basic kitchen utensils with which to prepare food for themselves. Records of ships arriving within 15 years after 1620 indicate that a quantity of cooking utensils as well as tools were brought from England to be sold or traded to the settlers. Forty-three years after the first settlers landed, a

Company of Undertakers for Iron Works was granted monopolies to manufacture iron for 12 years in Sangus (Lynn), Massachusetts. Under the direction of master mechanic John Jenks it produced pots, pans, nails, hinges, horseshoes, and other needed tools.[10] Artisans, craftsmen, tradesmen, skilled and semi-skilled workers were needed early on and were recruited to the colonies as early as 1629 as the need for manufactured tools was quite evident. Even the *Mayflower* had craftsmen aboard. From New Netherlands (New York) pamphlets were distributed in 1624 in England inviting craftsmen and tool workers to come and ply their trade or skills in the New World.

The New World's first English settlement was established on 19 May 1607 at Jamestown, Virginia. This settlement burned in 1608 but was rebuilt. By early 1609 the population was 550 people but the harsh winter of 1609 reduced the number to 65. In 1610 the settlement was abandoned but re-established under the management of the new governor, Lord Baltimore.

In the same year Henry Hudson sailed up the Hudson River to what is now known as Albany, New York. In 1612 the Dutch used Manhattan as a fur trading post and in 1614 John Smith explored, mapped, and named New England. The Little Harbor settlement in New Hampshire was established in 1623 by David Thomson and in the next year New Amsterdam was formally organized in what is now New York. In 1629 the Massachusetts Bay Colony was chartered and founded in 1630. Two years later Maryland was chartered. Thus these early settlements and explorations by the English firmly imposed an English character on the new lands. Later, colonies were settled in the South and what became known as the Middle Colonies opened the reality for the flood of immigrants to follow.

In New England in 1620–1621 many did not survive the severe winter. Their numbers increased the following year with the arrival of the ship the *Fortune* in November 1621. This ship was followed by others: *The Anne* and the *Little John* in August 1623, the *Sparrow* in March 1622, the second *Mayflower* in May 1629, the *Talbott* in July 1629, the *Handmaid* in October 1630, and in 1633 the *Straggling Saints* and *Merchant Adventure*. These ships brought a total of 362 new arrivals, 29 of which were artisans. In 1624 the population at Plymouth was about 180 persons, young and old. Without a doubt these new arrivals brought with them those items necessary to cook and prepare food. The artisans, most trained or involved with the preparing of wool for clothing, did include skilled craftsmen such as sawyers, smiths, printers, cabinetmakers, carpenters, shipwrights, masons, a nailer, a carriage maker, and coopers. The collective skills of these artisans enabled the community to build their homes and make the necessary tools. While it is uncertain how quickly these artisans were afforded an opportunity to employ their respective skills, they did have the knowledge to make trestle tables, wooden bowls, crude yet functioning fireplaces, simple looms, stools or benches, and implements to cultivate their gardens.

After the re-establishment of the colony at Jamestown, chartered as a commercial venture by English shareholders for tobacco, pine tar, and other native products, broadsides (posters) were published in London in 1622 advising those who contemplated emigration to the colony of what to bring with them. Listed were itemized clothes, victuals, arms, tools, and household implements.

Others writing back to England cautioned those who contemplated emigration to America to come with tools and cooking utensils. In 1630, Francis Higginson of Salem, Massachusetts, urged a family to bring "1 iron pot, 1 spit, 1 kettel, 1 frying Pan, 1 Gridiron, 2 Skettits, 1 spit, wooden Platters, Dishes, Spoons and Trenchers."[11] A writer of colonial times, Alice Morse Earle, reports having seen the underside of a trestle table made from wooden packing boxes or crates addressed to a settler in Boston in 1638 that indicated requests for supplies by the earliest settlers. Phipps also indicates that instructions for those who signed for passage by the Virginia Company in 1675 "were told that an iron pot, kettle, a large frying pan, a gridiron, two skillets, a spit, wooden platters, dishes and spoons were the amount of cooking equipments needed for each group of six."[12] Similar letters at later dates warned of the necessity of bringing utensils that were not readily available, especially inland from the coastal seaports. The lists accord fairly well with subsequent wills and inventories filed with probate courts.

Whatever the economic status of the early settlers—well-off-merchants, farmers, physicians or artisans—they all had more in common than they had differences. Phipps states, "The real contrasts are those of quantity: some simply had 'more of the same' than had their fellow colonists." At the turn of the eighteenth century the colonies had expanded and their cities had developed to such an extent that incoming immigrants could obtain needed kitchen utensils locally. Settlers on the frontier took only basic utensils.

In 1619, 800 indentured servants were imported to the Virginia Colony. In 1637, of the 2,675 immigrants, 2,094 were indentured servants. By 1640 the population of the Virginia Colony was about 8,000. It is doubtful the indentured servants brought all that was suggested since they immigrated largely in a destitute state. Akin to a peasant, indentured servants were required to serve five to seven years on a plantation and upon completion of their service the indentured servant was declared a freeman and entitled to 50 acres of land of his own. Owning property accorded him the right to vote.

In the New England region the Massachusetts Bay Colony was established in 1630 with religious dissenters and numbered 1,500. This colony was to some extent a commercial venture for its lumber and fish. England was at this time denuded of most of its forests because of the need to feed the huge fireplaces prevalent at the time and also because of the increasing demand for charcoal and coke to meet the demands for its iron foundries. Lumber, especially hard woods, was in great demand for shipbuilding and the constructing of homes and furniture. The colonies were rich in lumber and supplied England with this valuable resource. The Plymouth Colony existed until 1690 and then merged with the

Massachusetts Bay Colony. During the 1630s immigration to this new colony averaged about 2,000 people per year. Most of these new colonists settled in the Boston area, which became a major mercantile center. By 1670 the approximate population was 60,000 in Massachusetts alone, and by 1688 the total population of New England was about 75,000, settled mostly by people from East Anglia and southern England. Many of these were from London and its environs.

Throughout colonial times, the Atlantic coast colonies that had been chartered by the crown at the beginning of the seventeenth century continued to develop. Of note is the Chesapeake Region that included Maryland, Virginia, and northern North Carolina. North Carolina was settled specifically for economic gain from its abundant resources of tobacco as a cash crop, fish, pitch and pine tar, fur, coke, and minerals. The population in 1688 was about 75,000 and largely decentralized.

A polyglot of nationalities settled the Middle Colonies region composed of Delaware, New York, and New Jersey. This region was settled by Germans, Dutch, Scots-Irish, Swedes, and Finns and became the mercantile center of the New World. Early on fur was the principal trade in these colonies. Large tracts of cedar, black locust, and other hard woods also found a ready market in the developing colonies and in the home country.

Finns first settled in Delaware in 1636, but because they felt crowded they moved into the western parts of Pennsylvania and later into the mountains to the south. The Swedes called their place New Sweden and established a more permanent settlement in the Wilmington, Delaware area in 1638. The Dutch, already settled in the lower Hudson and Delaware River in 1623, located principally in New Amsterdam, later New York. In 1664 the English gained control of all Dutch holdings. Other nationalities assimilated into the larger English population. Pennsylvania was settled mainly by Quakers who were skilled artisans. Their settlements were soon augmented by settlers from the Palatinate, in the Rhineland, and by Moravians from Bohemia. Philadelphia became a major debarkation point for the Scots-Irish, Germans, and the English Quakers. The population of the Middle Colonies in 1688 was about 42,000. A wide variety of trades sprang up to satisfy the needs of the local communities. Farming was a major occupation providing produce to the growing cities.

One other area on the Eastern seaboard developed more slowly but later grew in significance as the cotton economy took hold after the invention of the cotton gin made cotton production profitable. The colonies of the South were southern North Carolina, South Carolina, Georgia, and Florida. Rice, indigo, sugar cane, and beef were the basis of the economy. Early immigrants were carefully selected for their physical condition and good character by the English landowners and overseers prior to embarkation. Owners of the land were largely wealthy aristocratic men residing in England who employed trusted overseers to manage the developing plantations. These overseers needed a large labor force, thus they imported slaves. By 1688 the estimated population of the southern colonies was 8,000, slaves not being counted. After 1660 all the colonies had a mixed ethnic population.

In his detailed study, Bernard Bailyn, a demographic historian, estimates "a total of at least 700,000"[13] or a yearly average of 4,500 immigrants entered British North America prior to 1760. This number includes 75,000 Germans and Swiss, 100,000 to 150,000 Scots-Irish. Of those arriving many were voluntary; however, a significant number came involuntarily. Slaves from Africa (about 175,000 in the same period) came not as people but as chattels, either already owned or as goods to be bought and sold. As the need for labor grew in the southern colonies, land speculators, ship captains, and "new landers" in the German principalities rounded up vagrants and the poor with false promises, drink, trickery, or by resorting to outright kidnapping to meet the demands for cheap labor in America. These unfortunates can hardly be expected to have brought much if anything in terms of worldly possessions to the New World.

By 1688 the total population of all the colonies had burgeoned to 200,000, not counting Native Americans, slaves, the Spanish, or the remnants of the French but including the French Huguenots. Settlements in the North centered in small villages and geographical features such as river junctions and seaports whereas in the South, with its open spaces and large plantations, families were widely spaced except in major commercial seaports such as Charles Town and Norfolk.

It should be noted that the different nationalities that settled in America came with their own native tongue. The Irish and the Scots spoke different dialects than the citizens of Yorkshire, Kent, or London. The Germans and the Dutch came speaking their own languages as did the French. Speakers of the Nordic languages such as the Finns, the Swedes, the Norwegians and other less represented nationalities all added to the wide variety of languages spoken in the colonies. Yet by 1776, 169 years or nine generations

after Sir Walter Raleigh founded Jamestown, almost all the immigrants in the New World were speaking English.

During the eighteenth century settlers saw a modest change in the quality of their homes, especially its household furnishings. More pewter, chinaware, and earthenware, a few luxuries, brass and copper kettles and pots found their way into the settlers' kitchens. The kitchen was still the center of the house with its large fireplace. Some householders built additions or ells for additional sleeping rooms or for the storage of food and harvested crops. However, one is cautioned against thinking that the majority of homes are as depicted in the restored buildings at Williamsburg, Virginia, or other show-like museum buildings of the period in New England. Most American homes were still simple and meagerly furnished as families were primarily concerned with their crops and cattle and providing food and basic necessities. The acquisition of land was an upmost priority in their lives. Ordinary families were using carved or turned bowls and cups made from chunks of maple and wild cherry and window lights from carefully shaved sheets of cattle horn. Peter Kalm, a Swede who traveled extensively in America in the mid-1700s, records that on 6 October 1747 he was in the Delaware River area of New Jersey, certainly not a frontier location, and notes the abundance of red maple wood "turned into plates, spools, feet for chairs and beds."[14] On 20 November 1747 while near Raccoon, New Jersey, he notes that the Indians used the laurel tree to make "spoons and trowels of its wood."[15] And on 13 December 1747 he describes with considerable care how the deciduous trees, namely oak and ash, were carved to make "dishes, [and] bowls"[16] by the Swedes and, more especially, by the Finlanders. He does add that at the time of his visit "the Swedes no longer make use of such bowls and dishes but earthen ware or vessels made of other wood." The Indians, according to Kalm, "made boilers and kettles of clay or of different kinds of potstone (Lapis ollaris)."[17] Rachel Feild in her *History of*

Cooking Equipment writes that in the early 1600s wooden dishes, especially serving bowls and platters, were made from beech and fruitwood such as apple or pear. Burrwood or the roots of trees were favored because the grain was not straight. Elm was seldom used as it warps and cracks due to changes in temperature and humidity, especially if used for making cheese or butter. Lime, alder, and sycamore wood was favored by a cooper for making butter-tubs and churns. Willow made good beating paddles and plungers. Rush, osier, and willow were plaited into mats and baskets for draining and packing butter and cheese. Mortars and pestles were made from *lignum vitae*, a very dense wood, cool as a stone and found in the West Indies.[18]

Kalm's travels from the Middle Colonies to upstate New York to Saratoga and on into Canada's Trois Rivieres (Three Rivers) and Quebec, offers an unparalleled insight to the houses, their contents, and the industries he encountered. By the mid-eighteenth century, although wealthy merchants, ship captains, military leaders, plantations owners, and shopkeepers in the major cities filled their homes with expensive imported furnishings from England, the general population could ill afford to acquire such fashionable imports. The influx of poor immigrants such as indentured servants, transported criminals, and previous immigrants in the seventeenth century were concerned primarily with survival. The British Crown forbade the colonies by law to establish industries. England wanted to control the flow of goods from her factories at high prices at the same time that her returning ships brought back essential raw material bought at very low prices. The Sugar and Stamp acts and the tax increases that began in 1763 all led to the revolution in 1776.

Yankee ingenuity prevailed. Farmers and settlers on land further west and even those in small villages, not having resort to the traders and the shops of the coastal regions, made do or improvised. Houses were often built without nails or other ironwork. Kitchen utensils were multi-purpose, clothes that wore out became strips to weave carpets, horn was soaked to become windows, and ashes were saved to make lye or soap. The forests were cleared by the practice of cutting almost through the trunks of many trees. Axing one tree through, it would fall on the others and like dominos the rest would fall. Thus necessity and prudence dictated the lifestyle of the colonists as they expanded into the wilderness.

Measures Standardized

The seventeenth- and eighteenth-century system of weights and measures seems confusing and highly inaccurate. The measuring devices used for various dry and liquid products were produced by hand and there was no bureau of standards as known today. There were officials appointed by the Crown in England to ensure that fair measure was given to the public. Penalties for false measurements were often a period of time in the pillory or closure of a business. Many measurements were made by eye. For weights, a degree of accuracy was achieved by the use of steelyard or scale, first recorded in 1639.

In 1790 France adopted the metric system. The U.S. Congress established uniform standards of weights and measures of ounces and pounds in 1836. This was a version of a British system that Britain had abandoned in 1824. A volumetric system for dry measure was not widely used until well into the nineteenth century in America, as testified by directions in surviving cookbooks. A scale for measurement by weight prevailed even for cakes and bread ingredients until around 1846. Eventually, a standard measurement for different products was adopted by governments—the barrel, bushel, butt, peck, quart, pint, gallon, cup, and the like; thus the terms became standard in England and America.

Change of Utensil Names

Important questions arise about the names of kitchen utensils used especially in the 13 colonies during the eighteenth century. Why did the English language prevail in the naming of utensils? Why did the names of some utensils become obsolete? Why did utensils' names change? Why did some early utensils cease to be used? And why did the spelling of some kitchen utensils become altered? Answers to these questions can only be speculative. An answer to the first question could be that the dominant language prevailed. For example, beginning with the mass movements of people at the end of the seventeenth century in Central Europe and England and also in America, dialect terms for some utensils were abandoned in favor of the terms the majority of the population used. For example, the term "trug," a dialect term from northern England, dropped out of usage as "wooden tray" was a more acceptable and descriptive term. Multiple terms for the same utensil also gave way to a term in more general usage. The Old English word "pin" for a small cask or keg ceased to be used as the words "cask" or "keg" became more universal. The Middle English term "broach" was dropped in favor of "spit." Standardization of terms began for items with similar functions although they might differ slightly in size, form, and material. Another factor of change seems to be the increase in trade between districts and nations. Merchants and traders favored use of a common, acceptable term to indicate accurate quantity that was essential to avoid confusion, particularly with measures.

Another reason for terms becoming obsolete has been the rapid change in the materials used in the making of the utensils and the evolution of kitchen tools. Several examples will serve to make this point. Early ovens were outdoor earthen bee-hive structures called "cloams." With the advent of ovens built into fireplaces and later into ranges or stoves, the earlier term was no longer applicable. The "black-jack," a term for a leather and tar jug or drinking vessel, gave way to the fired earthen pitchers, drinking vessels, and even later to glass. Ironware, hand-forged, heavy, and easily broken, was replaced with copper or brass pots and pans that in turn were largely replaced with tin-plated utensils or steel. The introduction of new processes for making utensils caused many earlier terms to become obsolete. The history of these new processes is well recorded.

With the population on the move and gathering in large numbers in cities and major trading centers, newer forms of production also brought about a loss of earlier terms.

Manufacturing burst on the scene in England and America in the late eighteenth century. Small utensils began to be made from rolled metal and stamping methods. No longer were wooden utensils laboriously shaped by hand. With the introduction of tin ware in Wales in 1720 utensils became lighter, not so easily broken, and could be mass-produced. Thus a cook had at hand a variety of fairly inexpensive utensils with which to prepare food. Innovations in the cooking process at the fireplace changed also. More efficient fireplaces were developed in which the intensity of heat could be controlled and utensils were adapted to these changes. The huge fireplaces of the sixteenth and seventeenth centuries became smaller and safer. In the nineteenth century the closed range or stove obviated the need for the many tools and utensils a cook needed at the fireplace. Thus the use and names of some utensils dropped from the common vocabulary.

Another factor of change was the expansion of trade. Items from the Far East—notably imports of chinaware from China—made for more sanitary conditions for the family as they replaced trenchers and communal drinking vessels. Possibly china plates, platters, and sauce dishes appealed to the owner's ego, because they gave an aesthetic quality to the dull and poorly lighted kitchen.

The industrial revolution that began about 1832 in England and later in America brought about real and significant changes in the utensils used in the preparation of food. Mass production, newer materials, novel manufacturing processes, increased trade, and plain old ingenuity brought about ease for the cook in the type of utensils used. The utility of a utensil was paramount. Even the flush of hundreds of utensils and dishes developed during the Victorian Age failed to alter the cook's use of utilitarian tools. The desire for lack of clutter and safer, cleaner utensils prevailed, so that today the sleek modern kitchen has reduced the time burden of food preparation. Improving the quality of food and offering a greater variety of dishes became the goal in most homes.

Kitchen utensils have had a long evolution. If progress can be measured by rapid changes, progress in the use and design of kitchen utensils was very slow. The cook of the year 1000 would not be unprepared to use the kitchen utensils of the late nineteenth and early twentieth centuries. Although the design may have changed and the material altered, the function of the tools remained essentially the same. Thus the cook could prepare the meal using the spatula, the pot, the pan, the long handled spoon, the cup, the kettle, and a host of other utensils that have remained relatively unchanged for 900 years. What the cook called each utensil did change, however, through the ill-understood process of language change. If the foundation of a good home is the kitchen, the kitchen is equally the foundation of humanity, for it is from the kitchen that mankind has obtained his sustenance through the centuries. What follows is a listing of the names of utensils and a general description. Some photographs and line drawings assist in providing a reader some idea of what the utensils looked like.

Utensils

SERVING DISHES

Term	Variant Spellings	Definition
bowl	bolla, bolle, boole, bol, boule, boul, bowle, boal, bole, bollan, bollen	A [round] vessel to hold liquids, rather wide than deep; distinguished from a cup, which is rather deep than wide. Usually hemispherical or nearly so. Distinguished from a basin in its more hemispherical shape.
burette	burett, buyret	A small cruet, [vial], or bottle for [oil] or vinegar.
cistern	cistetrne, cysterne, cistron, cestern(e), cestarne, systerne, sesterne, sestron, sestarne, sestur, sestourne, sisterne, systern	A large vessel or basin, often richly ornamented, used at the dinner-table.
charger	chargeour(e), charyowre, charyooure, charioure, chargiour, chargour, chargere	1. A large plate or flat dish for carrying a large joint of meat; a platter. 2. A large soup-plate or vessel for liquids.
losset	losad	A wooden tray.

Usage	Probable Source of Term and Cognates	Earliest Citation
	OE., MDu., Du., ON., OHG., MHG.	1000
Obs.	Fr.	1856
Obs.	OF., It., Pg., Sp.	1667
Obs.	OF., ME.	1305
Obs., dial.	OIr.	1645

Various sized trammels (a.k.a. pot hangers) for high cranes. Mercer Museum.

Term	Variant Spellings	Definition
maund		A basket made of wicker or other woven material, or (occas.) of wooden slats, with a handle or handles. (See also Measures.)
pap-boat	papp, pape, pappe	A boat-shaped vessel for holding pap for feeding infants. [Combination forms: pap-spoon, pap-bottle, pap-warmer.]
plate	plaate, platt, playte, pla(y)the, plaite, plat, plait, pleit, plet	1. A shallow, usually circular vessel, originally of metal or wood, now commonly of earthenware or china from which food is eaten. 2. [Table-ware; plates, dishes, etc.]
roundel	rondel, roundele, roundelle, roundill, roundul, roundall, roundal, roundale, rundle, rowndel, rowndell	A circular wooden trencher. [Both sides used to eat from. Cited in Harrison.]
saucepan		In early use, "a small deep skillet with a long handle, in which sauce or small things are boiled."
saucer	sawser(e), sawcer(e), sawsesere, sauscyre, sawssor, sowcer, saiser, salsar, salser, sausser, sawsser, sawecere, sasser, salcer, sasar, saser	1. A receptacle, usually of metal, for holding the condiments at a meal; a dish or deep plate in which salt or sauces were placed upon the table. 2. A small round shallow vessel, usually with concave sides and flat at the bottom, used for supporting a cup. 3. Any small shallow dish or deep plate of circular shape.

Usage	Probable Source of Term and Cognates	Earliest Citation
Loc., Appl., Spec.	OE., MDu., MG., MLG.	725
	MLG., LG., G., Du., OF.	1782
Obs.	OF., ME., Pg., Sp., It., LG., MDu., Du., MHG., Ger.	1450
Hist.	OF., MDu., Du., MLG., Ger., Da., Sw.	1797
		1686
Obs.	OF.	1489, 1607, 1702

Kitchen Utensils

Term	Variant Spellings	Definition
server	salver, salvor, servere, servar, servier	1. A spoon and fork for serving salad. [2. A dish on which a jelly or the like is served up for the table.]
trencher	trencheour, trenchour, trenchur, trenchor, trenchowre, threnshoure, trunschoure, trunschzour, trentcher, trunscheour	1. A flat piece of wood, square or circular, on which meat was served and cut up; a plate or platter of wood, metal, or earthenware. 2. A slice of bread used instead of a plate or platter. [Combination form: trencher-basket, trencher-bread (obsolete), trencher-knife (obsolete), trencher-plate.]
trug	trugg	A shallow wooden tray or pan to hold milk.
twiffler		A plate or shallow dish intermediate in size between a dessert plate and a dinner plate.

Usage	Probable Source of Term and Cognates	Earliest Citation
Obs.		1747–1796, 1884
Arch. & hist.	ONF., OF.	1308, 1380
Dial. var. of trough	NEng. dial.	1580
Hist.	Du.	1770

Square wooden trencher with carved depression in upper right corner for salt. Niina Aalto.

LIGHTING

Term	Variant Spellings	Definition
beam	baem, bem, beem, beme, beame	A candle
Betty lamp		[A shallow receptacle with a projecting nose an inch or two long filled with tallow or grease and a wick placed so that the lighted end could hang on the nose. Cited in Nutting.]
candle	condel, condell, candel, candell, kanndell, kandel, condle, condil, kandil, candelle, candylle, candulle, candul, cannel, cannele	A source of artificial light, usually consisting of a cylindrical body of wax, tallow, spermaceti, or other solid fat, formed round a wick of cotton or flax, formerly also, of the pith of a rush.
cresset-lamp	cresset-light, cresset-stone	[A flat stone with cup-shaped hollows for holding grease to be burnt for light.]
crusie	cruisie, crusy	A small iron lamp with a handle, burning oil or tallow. Also, a sort of

Usage	Probable Source of Term and Cognates	Earliest Citation
	OE., OFris., OSc., MDu., Du., OHG., MHG., Ger., WGmc., EGmc., Goth., ON.	1000
		1893
	OE., ME.	a700
		1875
	Fr., OF.	1774

Early hanging style Betty lamps. Mercer Museum.

Term	Variant Spellings	Definition
		triangular iron candlestick with one or more sockets for candles, having the edges turned up on the three sides.
extinguisher		A hollow conical cap for extinguishing the light of a candle or lamp.
iron cruses		[Same as Betty or Phoebe Lamp. Cited in Feild.]
link	linck(e), lynck(e), linke, lynk(e).	A torch made of tow and pitch (? sometimes of wax or tallow), formerly much in use for lighting people along the streets.
Phoebe lamp		[Similar to Betty lamp in shape. Some had double wicks from a nose on either side.]
ruff		A candle or candle-wick.
rush-candle		A candle of feeble power made by dipping the pith of a rush in tallow or other grease; a rushlight.
rush-holder		A device for holding a rushlight.
rushlight	rush-light	[A] rush-candle [or] the light of a rush-candle.

Usage	Probable Source of Term and Cognates	Earliest Citation
Spec.		1641
Obscure origin		1100
	N. Amer. hist.	1935
Obs.		1440
		1591
		1710

Kitchen Utensils

Term	Variant Spellings	Definition
save-all		A contrivance to hold a candle-end in a candlestick while burning so that it may burn to the end; a common form is a pan with a projecting pin in the cent[er] on which the candle-end is fixed.
slut	slotte, slute, slutte, slutt	A piece of rag dipped in lard or fat and used as a light.
snuff	snoffe, snof, snoff, snuffe, snuf	[An instrument used for snuffing out candles, etc.] [In later use only in the plural form.] That portion of a wick, that is partly consumed in the course of burning to give light, and in the case of candles requires to be removed at intervals.
spill	spille, spylle, spil	A thin slip of wood, a folded or twisted piece of paper, used for lighting a candle, pipe, etc.
splinter	splenter	Used as a torch, or dipped in tallow and used as a candle.

Usage	Probable Source of Term and Cognates	Earliest Citation
		1645
	Da., Norw., Sw.	1609
	Ger.	1382
		1821
	Du., MDu., LG., WFris., WFlem., Ger.	1751

Various sized trammels (a.k.a. pot hangers) for high cranes. Mercer Museum.

DRINKING VESSELS

Term	Variant Spellings	Definition
beaker	biker, becure, byker, bikyr, beeker	A large drinking vessel with a wide mouth, an open cup or goblet.
bellarmine		A large glazed drinking-jug with capacious belly and narrow neck.
bicker	biquere, biquour	A bowl or dish for containing liquor, properly one made of wood.
Black-Jack or black-jack		A large leather jug for beer, etc. coated externally with tar.
bombard	bumbard, boumbard, bombarde	A leather jug or bottle for liquor; a black-jack. [Other names for jugs: stone jug, flanders jug, tipt jug, Fulham jug.]
bowl	bolla, bolle, boole, boll, boule, boul, bowle, boal, bole	1. A [round] vessel to hold liquids, rather wide than deep; distinguished from a cup. 2. A drinking vessel. 3. The more or less bowl-shaped part of any vessel or utensil; *e.g.* of a cup or flagon, tobacco-pipe, spoon, candlestick, the scale-pan of a balance.

Usage	Probable Source of Term and Cognates	Earliest Citation
Chiefly in lit. use	ME., OHG., MHG., ON.	1348
Obs., hist.		1719
	Sc.	1458
	Eng.	1591
Obs., hist.		1596
	OE., MDu., Du., OHG., MHG.	1000

Kitchen Utensils

Term	Variant Spellings	Definition
caudle-cup	caudel, cawdel(l), cawdelle, cawdille, caudille, caudell, cadle, cawdale, cawdle, caudell	[A caudle-cup holding a hot drink, *e.g.*] of thin gruel, mixed with wine or ale, sweetened and spiced, given chiefly to sick people.
cruse	crowse, crowce, crewse, crwce, cruce, crouse, cruys(e), crewyse, cruze, criuze, creuse, cruise	A small earthen vessel for liquids; a pot, jar, or bottle; also a drinking vessel.
gispin	guispin, gyspen, gespen, gespin, gisken	A leathern pot or cup.
glass	glaes, gles, glas, glase, glasse, glaas, glasce, glace, glasshe	A glass vessel or receptacle. [Now] resembling a drinking glass.
goblet	gobelet, goblot, goblett, gublett, gobbelett, gobblet	1. A drinking cup of metal or glass, properly bowl-shaped and without handles, sometimes mounted on a foot and fitted with a cover. 2. A glass with a foot and stem, as distinguished from a tumbler.
horn	heorn, horun, horne	A vessel formed from the horn of a cow or other beast, or in times shaped after this, for holding liquid; a drinking-horn, hence a hornful; a draught of ale or other liquor.
madder	meader, mether, medder	A square wooden drinking vessel. [A wooden cup with handles and foot. Cited in Phipps.]

Usage	Probable Source of Term and Cognates	Earliest Citation
	ONF., OF.	1657
Arch.	Icel., Da., Sw., OHG., MHG., MLG., LG., MDu., Du., WFris., EFris., NFris.	1420
Obs.		1530
	OE., Du., OHG., MHG., Ger., OTeut., ON., Da., Sw.	1225
Arch.	OF.	1277
	OE., OFris., OSw., OHG., ON., OTeut.	1000
	AIr.	1720

Term	Variant Spellings	Definition
mazer	maser, mazere, mazre, maser(e), mausure, masour, masowyr, masar, masere, meyser, massor, masowyr, masser, masure, mazur, mazare, mazor	1. A maple or other fine-grained hardwood used as a material for making drinking vessels. 2. A bowl, drinking cup, or goblet, usually without a foot, [originally made of "mazer" wood, often richly carved or ornamented and] mounted with silver [and gold or other metal]. Frequently mounted with silver or silver gilt at the lip. Also: a similar vessel made of metal or other material.
mug	mugge	1. A drinking vessel, [usually] cylindrical, [with or without] a handle. 2. [Any (large)] earthenware vessel or bowl.
noggin	knoggin, noggan, naggin, nugging	1. A small drinking vessel; a mug or cup. 2. A pail or bucket.
quaich	quaigh, quegh, quaff, queff, quech, queich	1. A kind of shallow drinking-cup formally common in Scotland, usually made of small wooden staves hooped together and having two ears or handles, but sometimes fitted with a silver rim, or even made entirely of that metal. 2. A drinking vessel or trophy of similar design.
scale	skale, skaylle, scaile, skail, scole, scoale, skole, scoal, scowle, skoale	A drinking-bowl or cup.

42

Usage	Probable Source of Term and Cognates	Earliest Citation
Obs., hist.	OF., OHG., MHG., Du., ON.	1200, 1311
	LG., Norw.	1570, 1664
	Gael., Loc. U.S.	1630, 1885
	Gael., OIr.	1673
Obs.	ON., OHG., Sw., Da., MHG., ODu., OTeut., OE.	1205

Term	Variant Spellings	Definition
sneaker	sneak-cup	1. A small bowl (of punch). 2. A glass of brandy.
tankard	tancard, tankerd, tankarde, tankert, tanckerd, tanker	1. A large open tub-like vessel, usually of wood hooped with iron, etc. (sometimes of leather). 2. A drinking-vessel formerly made of wooden staves and hooped; now *esp.* a tall one-handled jug or mug, usually of pewter, sometimes with a lid; used chiefly for drinking beer.
taster	tastour, taastowre, tastar	A small shallow cup of silver, often with an embossed or corrugated bottom which reflects the light through the liquor, for tasting wine.
tumbler		A drinking cup, originally having a rounded or pointed bottom, so that it could not be set down until emptied, often of silver or gold; now, a tapering cylindrical, or barrel-shaped, glass cup without a handle or foot, having a heavy flat bottom.
tyg, tig		A name said to have been formerly given in the Straffordshire potteries to a porringer; now applied by antiquaries and collectors to a drinking cup with two or more handles, attributed to the 17th and 18th century.

Usage	Probable Source of Term and Cognates	Earliest Citation
Obs.		1700, 1805
Obs.	MDu., Du.	1310, 1485
	OF.	1420
		1664
		1838

Term	Variant Spellings	Definition
wassail-bowl		A large bowl or cup in which wassail [an alcohol drink] was made and from which healths were drunk; a loving-cup; also the liquor contained in the bowl.

Drinking Vessels

Usage	Probable Source of Term and Cognates	Earliest Citation
		1606

MEASURES

Term	Variant Spellings	Definition
anker	anchor	A measure of wine and spirits, used in Holland, North Germany, Denmark, Sweden, and Russia. It varies in different countries; that of Rotterdam, formerly also used in England, contains 10 old wine gallons or $8\frac{1}{3}$ imperial gallons. [Also] a cask or keg holding the above quantity. [Once used] as a dry measure of capacity [but now obsolete].
barrel	barayl, barele, barell(e), barel, barylle, barrelle, beryl, barrell	[A half hogshead.] 1. A cylindrical wooden vessel, generally bulging in the middle and of greater length than breadth, formed of curved staves bound together by hoops, and having flat ends or heads; a cask. 2. Used as a measure of capacity both for liquids and dry goods, varying with the commodity.
bole		Six bushels. Dry measure (oats, corn, barley, potatoes). [Zupko cites *OED*.]

Usage	Probable Source of Term and Cognates	Earliest Citation
	Du., Ger.	1597, 1673, c1750
	Pg., Sp., It., Med. L., Eng.	c1305, 1382

Term	Variant Spellings	Definition
bole		Four bushels. Dry measure (wheat or beans). [Zupko cites *OED*.]
bowl	bolle, boll, boull, bole, bow	A measure of capacity for grain, etc., used in Scotland and north of England, consisting in Scotland generally [of] 6 imperial bushels, but in the north of England varying locally from the "old boll" of 6 bushels to the "new boll" of 2 bushels. Also a measure of weight, containing for flour 10 stone [140 pounds]. [Cited in Zupko].
bushel	boyschel, buyschel, boissiel, buissiel, boisseau, boisteau	A measure of capacity used for corn, fruit, etc., containing 4 pecks or 8 gallons. [A]s a liquid measure [now obsolete.]
butt	butte, but	A cask for wine or ale, of capacity varying from 108 to 140 gallons. Afterwards also a measure of capacity = two hogshead, *i.e.* usually in ale measure 108 gallons, in wine measure 126 gallons; but these standards were not always precisely adhered to. 2. In wider sense: A cask or barrel.
chaldron	chauderne, chaudron, chawdron, chauldron, chalderon	[Measure for coal. In New York 2,500 pounds. In London 36 bushels.] A dry measure of 4 quarters or 32 bushels; in recent times only used for coals (36 bushels).

Usage	Probable Source of Term and Cognates	Earliest Citation
	ON., Da., OE.	1375
	ME., OF., F.	1300
	ME.	1443, 1626
	OF., F., Sp., It.	1555, 1615

Term	Variant Spellings	Definition
chopin	schopin, chopyn, choppyne, choppen, choppin, chopine, chappin	"A French liquid measure containing nearly a pint of Winchester," *i.e.* half an Old French *pinte*. A Scotch liquid measure, equal to a Scotch half-pint, or about a quart of English wine-measure.
cruskyn, cruisken	cruske, curskyn, crusisie	A small vessel for holding liquids; hence a liquid measure.
dram	dragm, drame	A fluid dram ($= \frac{1}{8}$ fluid ounce) of medicine. A small draught of cordial, stimulant, or spirituous liquor. [Combination forms: dram-cup, dram-glass, dram-bottle, dram-pot.]
firkin	ferdekyn, ferken, firken, fyrken, ferrekyn, firking, ferkin, firikin, firken	A small cask for liquids, fish, butter, etc., originally containing a quarter of a "barrel" or half a "kilderkin." [If a measure of butter 56 pounds. If liquid 8 to 9 gallons.]
firlot	ferlot, feirtot, fertot, ferthelett, fertleitt, furlet, fyrlot, furlot, farlet	A measure of capacity for corn, etc., the $\frac{1}{4}$ part of a boll. [Also] a vessel used to measure a firlot of corn, etc.
frail	frayel, fraell, fralle, fraiel, frayle, frale, fraile, freal	A kind of basket made of rushes, used for packing figs, raisins, etc., the quantity of raisins, etc. (30 to 75 pounds) contained in this.
gill	gille, jille, gylle, gyll, jill	1. A measure for liquids, containing one fourth of standard pint. In many

Usage	Probable Source of Term and Cognates	Earliest Citation
	F., Ger., LG.	1275
Obs.	OF., MFlem., Ir.	1378
	OF.	1674
	MDu.	1423
	ON., OE.	1264, 1573
	OF.	c1300
	OF.	1275, 1440

Term	Variant Spellings	Definition
		districts the gill is equivalent to a half-pint, the quarter-pint being called a *jack*. 2. A vessel holding a gill.
hogshead (wine)	hoggeshed, hoogeshed, hoggishede, hoggys hed, hogges heed, hoggesyde, hoggesheed, hoggis heed, hogyshed, hoggeshead, hogs(h)ed, hogsheed, hogs-head, hogs-hede, hogget, hoghead, hogheid(d), hogd-head	A large cask for liquids; hence, a caskful of liquor; a liquid measure. [In] 1423 [content] prescribed by a statute. The London hogshead of beer contained 54 gallons, that of ale 48 gallons; elsewhere the hogshead of ale or beer contained 51 gallons. (Now seldom used of beer, but almost invariably of cider.)
keelfat	kagles, keel-vat	A wooden tub; a keeler. A tub in which liquor is let to cool.
kilderkin	kynerkin, kynderkin, kynterkyn, kinderkind, kinderkin, kilderkyn, kylderkin, kylderkyn, kylderken	A cask for liquids, fish, etc. of a definite capacity (half a barrel).
lippie	leippie	[The fourth part of a peck; in goods sold by weight usually $1\frac{3}{4}$ lb. Cited in Zupko.]
measure	measur, mesour(e), measore, meser, myssour, myssuyr, meassour, missour	An instrument for measuring. A vessel of standard capacity used for separating and dealing out fixed quantities of various substances (as grain, liquids, [some vegetables,] coal).

Usage	Probable Source of Term and Cognates	Earliest Citation
	Flem., Du., MLG., LG., Ger., Sw., Da.	1390, 1392, 1483
		1552
	Du., LG., MDu.	1530
		1612
	Pr., Sp.	1297

Keelfat with ears. Author photo.

Term	Variant Spellings	Definition
moy		A dry measure of capacity, varying in quantity but usually amounting to several bushels, used *esp.* for salt. A measure used for salt; 15 bushels.
peck	pec, pek, pekke, peke, pecke, pect	A measure of capacity used for dry goods; the fourth part of a bushel, or 2 gallons. The imperial peck contains 554.548 cubic inches, that of the United States 537.6.
pin	pinn, pynne, pinne, pyn, pene, pyne, pynn, pine	A small cask or keg holding half a firkin, or $4\frac{1}{2}$ gallons.
pipe		[Two hogsheads.] 1. A large cask, of more or less definite capacity, used for wine, and formerly also for other liquids and provisions, or other goods. 2. A cask with its contents (wine, beer, beef, fish, etc.) or as a measure of capacity, equivalent to half a tun, or 2 hogsheads, or 4 barrels, *i.e.* containing usually 105 imperial gallons (= 126 old wine-gallons).
poke		A bag; a small sack: applied to a bag of any material or description, but usually smaller than a *sack*.
pottle	potel, potell, potelle, pottel(l), pottle	A measure of capacity for liquids (also for corn and other dry goods, rarely for butter), equal to 2 quarts of 1/2 gallon: now abolished. [Erroneous variant of bottle.]

Usage	Probable Source of Term and Cognates	Earliest Citation
	Fr.	1535
	ME., OF., AF.	1300
Obs.	OE., LG., MLG., MDu., Du., MHG., Ger., ON., Sw., Da.	1570
Obs.	OF., Fr. from Sp., Pg., It.	1392–1393
Dial.	ME., AL., ONF., Flem., Ir., Gael., Sc.	1276
Obs.	OF.	1300

Kitchen Utensils

Term	Variant Spellings	Definition
puncheon	roncion, pwncion, punchion, ponchion, poncheon, punshion, punchon, pontioune, puncioune, puncheoun, punsion, puns(i)oun, punschioun, puntion, punshon	A large cask for liquids, fish, etc.; *spec.* one of a definite capacity, varying for different liquids and commodities. As a liquid measure it varied from 72 (beer) to 120 (whisky) gallons.
quarter	quartare, quatteer, quartere, quartyer, wharter, qwarter, quartar, qwartter	One of four equal parts into which anything is or may be divided. The fourth part of a peck, cask, barrel, pound. The fourth part of a hundredweight = 28 pounds (*U.S.* commonly 25 lbs.)
quartern	quartron, quartrun, quartroun, quarteroun, quaterone, quateren, quarteron, quarteren, quartrone, quarterne, cartron, quartan, wartern	A quarter *of* anything or *of* something (*esp.* weight or measure) already specified.
quintal	quintale, quintell, kyntawes, kyntal, kyntayl, kintall, kintal, kentall, kental, kentle	A weight of one hundred pounds; a hundred-weight (112 lbs.). In the metric system: A weight of 100 kilograms.
ringe		1. [A smoothing iron.] 2. A large tub with two iron ears, containing 14 to 16 gallons, with which two servants fetch water from a distant place. [AKA: cowls.]

Usage	Probable Source of Term and Cognates	Earliest Citation
	Sc., OF.	1479
	OF.	c1400
Obs., dial.	AF., OF., Eng.	c1290
	OF., Sp., Pg., It., Med. L.	c1470
Dial.		

Term	Variant Spellings	Definition
roundlet	rownde, roundelet, roundelett, roundelete, rowndlet, rounlet, roundlett	A small cask; a runlet.
runlet	rondelet, rondlet, rundelet, rundlett, rundlet, ronlett, ronelete, runlett, ronlet, runlet, renlet(t)	A cask or vessel of varying capacity; the quantity of liquor contained in this. Large runlets appear usually to have varied between 12 and $18\frac{1}{2}$ gallons, small ones between a pint or quart and 3 or 4 gallons.
strike	strik, stryk, stryke	[One to four bushels.] A denomination of dry measure in various parts of England (but not officially recognized since the 16th century); usually identical with the bushel, but in some districts equal to a half-bushel, and in others to 2 or 4 bushels. Also, the cylindrical wooden measuring vessel containing this quantity.
trug		An old measure for wheat, equal to two-thirds of a bushel.
tub	tubbe, tobbe, tob, ytoubbe, tube, toob, tubb	1. An open wooden vessel, wide in proportion to its height, usually formed of staves and hoops, of cylindrical or slightly concaved form, with a flat bottom. 2. A small cask or keg of spirit, containing about 4 gallons. (A smuggler's term.)

60

Usage	Probable Source of Term and Cognates	Earliest Citation
Obs.	OF.	1388
Arch., hist.	OF.	1394
	MLG.	1284
	Eng.	1350
	ME., MDu., MLG., MFlem., WFris., LG.	1386

FIREPLACE AND FIREPLACE TOOLS

Term	Variant Spellings	Definition
andiron	aundyre, aundyrne, aundiren, awndyryn, aundeiren, aundryn, andyron, awnderne, andyar, awndyrn, aundyern, aundyron, aundernn, handern, handiron, hnadyron, landyron	A utensil, consisting of an iron bar sustained horizontally at one end by an upright pillar or support usually ornamented or artistically shaped, at the other by a short foot; a pair of these, also called "*fire dogs*," being placed, one at each side of the hearth or fire-place, with ornamental ends to the front, to support burning wood. Sometimes "in a kitchen fire-place the upright support carried a rack in front for the spit to turn in." [AKA: cob-irons, brand-irons, spit-dogs, fire-dogs, hand-iron, staukes, cup dogs.]
ash	aesc, asse, aychs, assch(e) asch(e), assh(e), ashe, aish, esche, ach	[Combination forms:] **ash-bin**, a receptacle for ashes and household refuse; **ash-box**, a receptacle for ashes; a pan beneath a fire-grate; **ash-pan**, a utensil (fitted with a grate) in which the ashes are collected and removed; **ash-oven**.

Usage	Probable Source of Term and Cognates	Earliest Citation
		1300
Chiefly U.S.	OE., ON., OHG., MHG., Ger., OTeut.	1846

Kitchen Utensils

Term	Variant Spellings	Definition
axe	acas, äx, eax, aex, (echze), ex(e), aix, ax	A tool or instrument for hewing, cleaving, or chopping trees, wood, ice, etc.; consisting of a squarish head, now usually of iron with a steel edge or blade, fixed by means of a socket upon a handle or helve of wood, so as to be wielded with force in striking.
batling		A small stick, a faggot.
beehive-oven		[Combination form: beehive-oven] in sense of shaped like a bee-hive. [Cited in Phipps.]
bellows	beli, bely, belies, bulies, belyes, belise, belice, bales, bellies, bellyis, belw, belu, below, bel(i)owe, belwes, belwis, belwys, belowys, bellowse, bellowes	An instrument to furnish a strong blast of air[,] to blow a fire; may be portable or fixed.
besom	besma, besema, besem, besme, beesme, bisme, besum, besumme, bessume, besowme, besome, bysom, beasome, bessem, beesom(e), beesum, beasom, boosome, bissome, bezom, bizzim, buzzom	An implement for sweeping, usually made of a bunch of broom, heather, birch, or other twigs bound together round a handle; a broom. (Dialectally, as in Scotland, the generic name for sweeping implements of any material, *e.g.* a *heather, birch*, or *broom besom*, a *hair besom;* but in literary Eng. "broom" is now generic, and "besom" specific.)
brand tongs		[Metal tongs used to pluck a hot coal from fire to light a rush light or candle. Cited in Phipps.]

Usage	Probable Source of Term and Cognates	Earliest Citation
	OE., OSw., MDu., Du., OHG., MHG., Ger., ON., Goth.	c1000
Dial., rare		1864
		1881
	OE., Sw., Da., ME.	800
	OE., OFris., OHG., MHG., Ger., Du.	c1000

Term	Variant Spellings	Definition
brander	brandyr, brandreth, brandire, brandise	A variant of brand-iron, a gridiron.
brandiron	brandhirne, braneyrne, branerne, branyren, brond-iron	A kitchen utensil, commonly a gridiron, but the name is transferred to other articles, as andirons (still *dial.* in Kent), a stand for a kettle, a trivet.
brandreth	branderith, brandryt(h)(e), brandrethe, brandrate, brandereth, brandreth, brandrith, brandelede, branlet, breniede, brandelette	A gridiron; a tripod or trivet of iron. (Originally a grate supported on three legs on the hearth: hence the apparent variety of definitions.)
bridge	brycg, bricg, brugge, brygge, bregge, brigge, brudge, bryg, bridg, brudge, brig, brygg, bregg, brigg	Applied to various utensils of more or less bridge-like form, *e.g.* a tripod for holding a pot over a fire.
broach	broche, brotche, broch, brooch, brotch	[An iron] pointed instrument used for roasting meat upon; a spit.
broiler		A gridiron or similar utensil used in broiling.
chamber grate		A cast-iron grate used for burning coal. [AKA: cole basket.]
clavel	cavie, clavy, clavey, cavel	The lintel over a fire-place; *esp.* a beam of wood so used, the mantel
cloam	clam, clome, cloame, cloume, clomb	Mud, clay, [or] earthenware. [Cloume ovens are earthen ware of several sizes, like an oven, and being heated they stopped them up and covered them over with embers to keep in the heat. Cited in Poccke Trav (cornw.) (1888).]

Usage	Probable Source of Term and Cognates	Earliest Citation
Obs.	Sc.	1450
Obs.		1381
Obs., dial.	ON., OE., OHG.	1400
Dial.	OE., OFris., MLG., MDu., Du., OHG., MHG., Ger., OTuet.	1847–1878
Obs.	ME.	1400
Now U.S.	F.	1393
		1600
Obs., dial.	OF.	1602
Obs.	OE., MDu., ON., OHG., MDu., WGmc.	1000

Brandreth (a.k.a. gridiron, tripod, trivet) Approx. 3 inches in height. Author photo.

Four brandreths or trivets. Sat on fireplace coals or hearthstone for holding a posnet or frying pan. Mercer Museum.

Kitchen Utensils

Term	Variant Spellings	Definition
cobbit	cobarde, coberte, coberd	Two iron bars at the upper end to rest upon the andirons; meeting at the opposite extremity on the hearth, they form a kind of cradle for the firewood.
cob-iron	cobiren, cobern, cobborne, cobyron, cobb-iron, cobiron	"One of the irons on which a spit turns"; "the irons hung on the bars of the kitchen-range to support the spit." Also [an] andiron; but cob-irons and andirons are distinct in early inventories.
cooker		A stove or other apparatus designed for cooking. A vessel in which food is cooked.
cotterel	cotterell, cotteril(l), cottrel, cottreil, kotrell	A trammel, crane, or bar, from which a pot or kettle is hung over a fire.
cradle spit		[A long rod resting on fire dogs with a basket for roasting smaller joints of meat or poultry. Cited in Kauffman.]
crane	cran, cron, krane, crone, cren, craane, crayne, craune, craine, crain	An upright revolving axle with a horizontal arm fixed by a fireplace, for suspending a pot or kettle over the fire. [AKA: reckons, sway.]
curfew	coeverfu, corfu, corfew, curfewe, curfu, courfeu, curpheue, curfue, curphew, corfeu, corfue, corphew, curfeu, corfour, curfur, courfyre, curfoyr, curfure, curphour, curfle, couvrefeu, coverfeu, coverfew	A cover for a fire; a fire-plate, a cover-fire.

Usage	Probable Source of Term and Cognates	Earliest Citation
Dial.		c1425
Obs.		1485
		1884
Southern dial.		1570
	MDu., Du., MGer., MLG., OHG., OLG., OE., MHG.	1864
	OF.	1626

Various kettles suspended by trammels from crane or lug pole. In foreground a hastener. Mercer Museum.

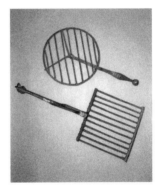

On left a swivel-type hearth gridiron (a.k.a. cast iron whirling broiler). On right a simple hearth gridiron that would rest on a bar spit. Used for broiling fish, meat or toast bread. Mercer Museum.

Kitchen Utensils

Term	Variant Spellings	Definition
dangle spit		[A metal hook attached to a string from which attached meat could be spun before or over a fire for roasting. Cited in Feild.]
dog-grate		A detached fire-grate standing in a fireplace upon supports called dogs. [AKA: andiron.]
dosser	doser, docer(e), dossour, dosour, dosur(e), dossar, dorser, dorsere, dorcere, dorsur, dorsour, dorcer, dorsar, doreur	An ornamental cloth used to cover the back of a seat, *esp.* of a throne or chair of state, or as a hanging for the wall of a hall or room of state, or of the chancel of a church. [AKA: a fire-back in a fire-place. Cited in Feild]
fender		A metal frame placed in front of a fire to keep falling coals from rolling out into the room.
fetter	feoter, feter, fetor, fet(t)re, vetre, feder, fettir, fetrer, fettar, fettour, fettyr, fetur	A chain or other apparatus by which cooking vessels are suspended over a fire; now usually a vertical bar pierced with holes, into one of which the pot-hook is inserted.
fire-back		The back wall of a furnace or fireplace. [Fire-backs of fireplaces have often been made separate.]
fire-basket		A receptacle used to hold fuel, *esp.* coal or wood for the fireplace. [Combination form: fire-bag,

Usage	Probable Source of Term and Cognates	Earliest Citation
		1881
Obs.	OF.	478
		1688
Obs.	OE., Du., OHG., MHG., ON., Sw., OTeut.	1400
		1847

Dangle spit. Weights at top ends help a continued spin. Niina Aalto.

Small posnet suspended from trammel from lug pole. Author photo.

71

Term	Variant Spellings	Definition
		fire-basket, fire-cage, fire-chauffer.] A portable grate.
fire-dogs		[Another term for andiron.] A similar support for a dog grate or stove. A rest for the fire-irons.
fire iron		An iron (or a steel) for striking a light.
fire-pan		1. A pan or receptacle for holding or carrying fire, *e.g.* a brazier, a chafing dish, a portable grate. 2. A pan for heating anything over a fire. *Obs.* 3. A tinder box. 4. A pan for carrying hot coals.
fire-pike		An instrument for stirring or making up a fire.
footman		A stand to support a kettle, etc. before a fire. [An iron or brass-and-iron trivet placed beside a fire in the dining room or parlor to hold dishes and plates to keep them warm. Cited in Feild.]
gallow(s)-balk	gally-bauk, galley-baak, galley-bawk, gallibauk, gally-balk	The iron bar in a chimney from which the pot-hooks hang.
gawberd	gawbert, gawberte, gaubert	Iron racks for chimneys.
gib	gibbe, gibb	An iron hook [pot hook]. [Combination form: gib-crook, gib-staff, gib stick.]

Usage	Probable Source of Term and Cognates	Earliest Citation
	OF., Fr.	1300
Obs.		
		1000, 1607
		1413
Rare or dial.		1767
Obs.		1583
Obs.		1520
Obs.		1567

Kitchen Utensils

Term	Variant Spellings	Definition
grate	gratte	A frame of metal bars for holding the fuel in a fireplace or furnace. Hence, the fireplace itself. [Combination form: grate-fire, grate-iron = gridiron.]
hatchet	acas, äx, eax, aex, ex(e), aix, ax, axe, axes	A smaller or lighter axe with a short handle, adapted for use with one hand. A tool or instrument for hewing, cleaving, or chopping, trees, wood, ice, etc.; consisting of a squarish head, now usually of iron with a steel edge or blade, fixed by means of a socket upon a handle or helve of wood, so as to be wielded with force in striking, Also called, especially when of a smaller or lighter make, a hatchet.
hake	haik, hage, haak, haken	1. A hook, *esp.* a pot-hook. 2. A wooden frame suspended from the roof for drying cheeses; a wooden frame for holding plates.
hastener		A stand or screen for concentrating the heat of the fire on a roasting joint of meat.
hob	hub	1. In a fire-place, the part of the casing having a surface level with the top of the grate. It appears to have been a boss or mass of clay behind the fire, the "back of the chimney" or "grate"; afterwards, the brick or stone back and sides of a grate; now, usually, the iron-plated sides of a

Usage	Probable Source of Term and Cognates	Earliest Citation
	OF.	1605
	OE., OSw., MDu., Du., OHG., MHG., Ger., ON., Goth.	c1000
Dial.	ON., Sw., Da., MDu., Du., Ger.	1488, 1768
Dial.		1847–1878
		1511

Term	Variant Spellings	Definition
		small grate, on which things may be set to warm. 2. [A trivet with four legs. Cited in Feild.]
hook	hoc(hooc), hoc, hok, hoke, houk, howk, huke, hooke, hoocke, hwick	A length of metal, or piece of wood or other material, bent back, or fashioned with a sharp angle, often forming a part of something, as a pole, chain, etc., adapted for catching hold, dragging, sustaining suspended objects, or the like. (Frequently with a qualification indicating shape or use, as *chimney-hook*, *clip-hook*, *fire-hook*, *flesh-hook*, *meat-hook*, *pot-hook*.)
jack	Iakke, Iacke, Iak, Iack, Jack	A machine for turning the spit in roasting meat; either wound up like a clock or actuated by the draught of heated air up the chimney (*smoke-jack*).
jib	gib	The projecting arm of a crane [in a fireplace]. [AKA: cotralls, cotrails, jib-hooks, hangers, trammels. Cited in Phipps.]
kitchner		[A cooking range fitted with various appliances such as ovens, plate-warmers, water heaters, etc. Cited in Harrison.]
lazy-back, idle back		[A bent iron or other metal open frame attached to a pot or kettle to prevent burning hands when removing such from a fire. AKA: kettle tilter, lazy

Usage	Probable Source of Term and Cognates	Earliest Citation
	OE., MLG., MDu., Du., MLG.	900
	ME.	1587
		1851

Utensil to withdraw hot dishes from fireplace oven. Niina Aalto.

Term	Variant Spellings	Definition
		Susan, lazy Betty, tipper, lazy elbow. Cited in Feild.]
lug-pole	log-pole	1. A long stick or pole; the branch or limb of a tree. [2. A (green) log at or near the inside top of fireplace opening from which pot-hooks and chains were hung. Cited in Carlo.]
lum	lumbe, lume, lumb	A chimney; also a chimney-top
malkin, mawkin	malekin, malkyn, malkyne, maulkin, maulken, malkine, malking, molkin, makin, maukyn, mawkine, maukin, mauking, mawking, maulmy, malmy	A mop; a bundle of rags fastened to the end of a stick, *esp.* [that used to clean] out a baker's oven.
oven	ofn, ofen, ouen, ouene, houen, ovuen, oven(n)e, ovon, owen, owyn, ovyn(e), oueen, oyne, hoyne, une, oon	1. A chamber or receptacle of brick, stonework, or iron, for baking bread and cooking food, by continuous heat radiated from the walls, roof, or floor. 2. *Dutch oven*, (*a*) large pot heated by surrounding it with fuel, and placing hot coals on the lid; (*b*) a cooking utensil made of sheet-metal, placed in front of a grate and heated by radiation and by reflection from the back of the chamber.
pawn	pan	[Usually a valance hung on the edge of mantle-shelf. Cited in Earle.]

Usage	Probable Source of Term and Cognates	Earliest Citation
		1773
		1697
Obs.	ME.	1440
	OE., OLG., MLG., MDu., Du., OHG., MLG., Da., ONorw.	1000
	Mainly of Du. origin	1578

Term	Variant Spellings	Definition
range		A form of fire-grate, fire-place, or cooking apparatus. Hence, a fire-place having one or more ovens at the sides, and closed on the top with iron plates having openings for carrying on several cooking operations at once. Also, a gas or electric cooker, typically with a grill, ring burners or plates, and one or more ovens.
reredos	rerdos(e), rerdoos(e), reredosse, reredoos, reredose, reredoce, reredes, reredoyse, reredorse, reredos, reyredewse, reerdos, rardros, rardess, reardashe, reardorse, redoce, redoss, redoes, redrosse, reddos	The brick or stone back of a fire-place or open hearth; an iron plate forming a fire-back.
scavel	scavell, skavell, skavel, skeval, skafell, skaffel, scaffle	1. A small spade. 2. [It differs from a spade in not tapering toward the edge, and in having its sides slightly turned up. Cited in Moor, *Suffolk Wds.*] [Also a shovel.]
shovel	scofl, scobl, ssofle, schovele, schovel, schofylle, schovyl(le), schowulle, schowuelle, shofful, showele, shovele, shoville, schovell, shovill, shovell, schovyll, shoffell, choffell, shoovell, shovull, shovelle, showel, showell, shufle, schule, schoyll, schwll, schowle, sholl, shole, schuill, showll, shoull, shiowle, showle, schole, shoule, shule, shull, shool, shoo, shoul, showl, shul, scolf, chollve	A spade-like implement, consisting of a broad blade of metal or other material attached to a handle and used for raising and removing quantities of earth, grain, coal or other loose material. [AKA: baker's shovel = peel.]

Usage	Probable Source of Term and Cognates	Earliest Citation
Now chiefly U.S.		1446–1447
Obs.	AF.	1392
Dial.	ON.	1440, 1823
	OE., MHG., LG., MDu., Du., MSw., Da., Norw., OHG., MHG., Ger., NFris., OTeut.	725

Term	Variant Spellings	Definition
smoke-jack		An apparatus for turning a roasting spit, fixed in a chimney and set in motion by the current of air passing up [the chimney].
smoke shelf		[A shelf built into back or side of fireplace to keep foods hot. AKA: channel, a hob. Cited in Feild.]
spill	spille, spyll(e), spil	A thin slip of wood, a folded or twisted piece of paper, used for lighting a candle, pipe, etc.
spit	spitu, spite, spyte, spete, speete, speet, speit, speite, speitt, speat, speate, speet, spet, spette, spitte, spitt, spytt(e), spyt	A cooking implement consisting of a slender sharp-pointed rod of metal or wood, used for thrusting into or through meat which is to be roasted at a fire; a broach. [Combination forms]: **spit-rack**, a spit with a turning mechanism; **spit-rack**, a rack used for supporting a spit or spits; **spit-turner** (obs.), a device for turning a spit; **spit-wheel** (obs.), a wheel serving to turn a spit.
sway	sweighe, sweigh, swey, swegh, sweyh, swey, sweygh, swale, swaye, swaigh(e), swea, suey, suai, swee, swye	A flat iron rod suspended in the [back of the] chimney on which [were hung iron hooks or chains with hooks to hang] pots [or] kettles. [AKA: reckons.]
trammel		A series of rings or links, or other device, to bear a crook at different heights over the fire; the whole being

Usage	Probable Source of Term and Cognates	Earliest Citation
		1675
		1821
	MDu., Flem., Du., MLG., LG., OHG., MHG., MSw., Da., WFris.	1000
	Sc.	1825
Now local Eng. and U.S.		1537

Hanging Betty lamp. Niina Aalto.

Iron toddy stick. Niina Aalto.

83

Term	Variant Spellings	Definition
		suspended from a transverse bar (the crook-tree), built into the chimney, or from a small crane or gallows, the vertical member of which turns in sockets in the jamb and lintel.
turnspit		1. [Combination form:] A dog kept to turn the roasting-spit by running within a kind of tread-wheel connected with it. 2. A boy or man whose office was to turn the spit. 3. [Combination forms:] A roasting-jack. turnspit-boy, turnspit-cur, turnspit-jack, turnspit-terrier.
worm	wyrm, wirm(e), wrim, wyrme, weorm, werm, werme, wurm, wurem, wurrm, wrm, wourme, woirme, woorme, worme	1. A long spiral or coiled tube connected with the head of a still, in which the vapour is condensed. 2. A spiral heating flue in a furnace or coiled steam pipe in a boiler. Terms used to describe various receptacles for burning fuel: fire-bag, fire-basket, fire-cage, fire-chauffer. Terms pertaining to the fire of a hearth or furnace: fire-bellows, fire-block, fire-blower, fire-brush, firecheek, fire-cricket, fire-door, fire-grate, fire-nook, fire-rake, fire-set, fire-stock, fire-stove.

Usage	Probable Source of Term and Cognates	Earliest Citation
		1576

Stationary trammel with adjustable crane. At left, a small slice or peel. Author photo.

Usage	Probable Source of Term and Cognates	Earliest Citation
	MHG., LG., MDu., Du., LHG., Ger., ON., Sw., Da., Norw.	1641, 1758
		1475–1756

An unusual wall-mounted tin oil lamp. Author photo.

HOUSEHOLD

Term	Variant Spellings	Definition
ale-shoe		[A vessel into which a hot iron is placed to heat ale. Cited in Phipps.]
bakestone	bakstone, backstone	A flat stone or slate on which cakes are baked in the oven; a plate of iron used for the same purpose. [A griddle.]
banker	bancour, banquer(e), bankewere, bankqwer, banwher, banckwarre, bankard, bynker	A covering, generally of tapestry, for a bench or chair.
bannock-stick, bannock board	bannuc, bannok, bannack, bannock	A wooden roller for rolling out bannocks [on a bannock-stone or a bannock board, a home-made bread, usually unleavened, of large size, round or oval form, and flattish. In Scotland usually made of barley or pease-meal but may be made of wheaten flour. In north of England sometimes (made of) oat or haver-bread.]
basin	bascin, bacin, bacine, bcyn(e), bassyn(e), basyn, basson, bassyng,	A circular vessel of greater width than depth, with sloping or curving sides,

Usage	Probable Source of Term and Cognates	Earliest Citation
Dial.		1531
Arch.	AF.	1311
Dial.	Gael.	1800
	ME., OF., Pg., Sp., OHG., Ger., Du.	1220

Ale shoe. Niina Aalto.

Hanging baking iron which hung from a trammel. Niina Aalto.

 87

Term	Variant Spellings	Definition
	bassien, bacen, bayseyn, bassine, basing, baiseing, basen, bason	used for holding water and other liquids, especially for washing purposes. [Wash bowls or basins are large, whereas breakfast bowls or basins are small. Cited in Carlo.]
beam		[A barrel. A tub. Cited in Phipps.]
beater		An instrument or contrivance for beating. Generally, an implement for beating flat or pounding [as in a mortar].
becket		[A rope handle. Cited in Phipps.]
bittle	betill, beetle	A obs. form of **beetle**. A mallet, a kitchen implement for bruising barley, mashing potatoes.
bittlin		[A milk pail or a milk bowl of wood, pewter, glass, or pottery. Cited in Phipps.]
blancmange	blancmanger, blankemanger, blancmangere, blamanger, blammanger, blanmanger, blaumanger, blamyngere, blanc maungere, blaunche-manger, blonc-manger, blawemanger, blanger mangere, blowmanger, blanchmanger, blanckmanger, blomange, blamange	Formerly a dish composed usually of fowl, but also of other meat, minced with cream, rice, almonds, sugar, eggs, etc. [Now] obs. Now a sweetmeat made of dissolved isinglass or gelatine boiled with milk, etc., and forming an opaque white jelly; also a preparation of cornflower and milk, with flavoring substances [served in a cup].

Usage	Probable Source of Term and Cognates	Earliest Citation
		1611
		Late 15th century
	OF.	1377

Term	Variant Spellings	Definition
bleeding-bowl		The so-called Bleeding Bowl, or Cupping Dish. [Such bowls were used by surgeons when bleeding their patients. Quoted in *Connoisseur*, Dec. 229/2, by Jackson, in *OED*.] [AKA: a taster.]
boulter	bulture, bultar, bulter, bowter, bultre, boultar, bolter	A piece of cloth used for sifting; a sieve, strainer; a bolting machine. [Combined forms: bolt-cloth, bolt feeder, bolt-poke.]
bovinizer		[A meat tenderer. AKA: a beetle (fret) or steak pound or meat fret or steakgreith. Cited in Feild.]
bread tester or cheese taster		[A slender plunger of metal that is thrust into food to draw out samples. Cited in Phipps.]
broiler		A gridiron or similar utensil used in broiling.
buck	bucke, bouke, bouck, book, bock	1. A washing tub, a vat in which to steep clothes in lye. 2. A quantity of clothes, cloth, or yarn, put through the process of bucking, in buckwashing or bleaching. [Combination forms:] ***buck-basket***, **buck ashes**, ***buck-vat***, **buck-house**, **buck-lye**, ***buck-sheet***.
buck-washing	buck-washer, buck-wash	The process of washing coarse and very dirty linen, by boiling it in an alkaline lye and afterwards beating and rinsing it in clear water.

90

Usage	Probable Source of Term and Cognates	Earliest Citation
		1911, 1916
	OF.	1440
Chiefly U.S.		1393
Obs.	OE.	1530
Obs.		1598

Hand-carved wooden spoons and mallet. At right, iron hook to remove dishes from fireplace oven. Author photo.

Term	Variant Spellings	Definition
can	canne, cane, kan, kanne, cann	A vessel for holding liquids; formerly used of vessels of various materials, shapes, and sizes, including drinking vessels; now generally restricted to vessels of tin or other metal, mostly larger than a drinking-vessel, and usually cylindrical in form, with a handle over the top.
canister	cannister	A small case or box, usually of metal, for holding tea, coffee, shot, etc.
case bottle		A bottle, often square, made to fit into a case with others. A bottle protected by a case.
castor	caster, cast	A small vessel with a perforated top, from which to cast or sprinkle pepper, sugar, or the like, in the form of powder; extended to other vessels used to contain condiments at table, as in "a set of casters," *i.e.* the castors and cruets usual in a cruet-stand.
cellar	celer(e), seler, celler, celar, seller, sellar, sellor	A box, a case; *esp.* for holding bottles; a case of bottles. (For salt-cellar cf. saler, of which *-celler* is a corruption).
chamber-utensil		[Chamber-vessel =] chamber pot.
chessel	cheswell, chessil	A cheese-vat. [The curds are put into the chessel or cheese-mould, which is placed under the press. Cited by Forsyth, 1805.]

92

Usage	Probable Source of Term and Cognates	Earliest Citation
	OE., WGmc. MDu., Du., MHG., ON., Sw., Da., OTeut.	1000
	Gr.	1711
		1719
		1676
Obs.	ME., AF., OF.	1632
		1721, 1805

Kitchen Utensils

Term	Variant Spellings	Definition
chopper		An instrument used for cleaving or cutting up: *spec.* a large-bladed short-handled axe used for cutting up meat, wood, etc.; a butcher's cleaver.
churn	cyrin, kyrne, chyrne, chirne, charne, cherne, chearme, churm(e)	A vessel or machine for making butter, in which cream or milk is shaken, beaten, and broken, so as to separate the oily globules which form the butter from the serous parts.
colander, cullender	colonur, colyndore, colendre, collandar, colender, colander, colinder, colendar, cullyandre, cullyinder, cullyander, cullyendar, cullyender	A vessel, usually made of metal, closely perforated at the bottom with small holes, and used as sieve or strainer in cookery.
costrel	costril(le), costrele, costrylle, costerell, kostorell, castrel, costril	A vessel for holding or carrying wine or other liquid; a large bottle with an ear or ears by which it could be suspended from the waist (whence the antiquarian designation "pilgrim's bottle"), or a small wooden keg similarly used, in which sense it is still in dialect use.
coul, cowl	cuvel, coules, couel(e), kouuele, kowuele, cowuele, cowle, coule, coole, kowle	A tub or similar large vessel for water, etc.; *esp.* applied to one with two ears which could be borne by two men on a cowl-staff.
cowl-staff, coul-staff	cuuel-staff, coule-staff, cowle, cole-staff, coal-staff, coole-staff, col-staff, coll-staff, colt-staff	A stout stick used to carry a "cowl," being thrust through the two handles of it; a pole or staff used to carry burdens, supported on the

Usage	Probable Source of Term and Cognates	Earliest Citation
		1818
	OE., MGer., LG., MDu., Du., ON., Da., Sw.	1000
	It., Fr., Sp.	1450
Obs., dial.	OF., med. L.	a1400
Arch. or dial.	ME., OF., Fr., OE., MHG., OHG.	1250
Arch. and dial.		1250

Kitchen Utensils

Term	Variant Spellings	Definition
		shoulders of two bearers; a "stang." It was formerly a familiar household requisite, and a ready weapon.
creel	crele, creille, crelle, creil, krele, kreil, creele, crail	1. A large wicker basket; formerly applied to the large deep baskets, coupled in pairs across the backs of horses, for the transport of goods; now applied to a basket used for the transport of fish and borne upon the back. 2. [In] spinning a frame for holding the paying-off bobbins in the process of converting the "sliver" into "roving," or the latter into yarn. Hence also **creel-frame.**
crimper		The name of several instruments used in crimping. An apparatus consisting of a pair of fluted rollers, for crimping cloth or the like.
crock	crocca, krocke, crocke, crokk(e), crok	An earthen pot, jar, or other vessel.
crotch	croche	A forked peg or crook for hanging things on.
cruet	curette, cruete, crowet, crowette, crewyt, kreweyye, crwett, crewett, cruat, cruytte, crewat, crowat, crouette, cruit, creuett, crewet	A small bottle or vial for liquids, etc.; now only applied to a small glass bottle with a stopper, to contain vinegar, oil, etc. for the table.

Usage	Probable Source of Term and Cognates	Earliest Citation
	Sc.	1425
		1877
	OE., Da., Sw.	1000
Obs.		1573
	ME., OF., OLG., MLG., OHG.	1382

Term	Variant Spellings	Definition
custard filler		[A wooden long-handled utensil used to fill pastry cases with egg and milk mixture and then inserted into a bee-hive oven for baking. Cited in Feild.]
dasher		That which dashes; *spec.* the contrivance for agitating the cream in a churn. [A plunger.]
decanter		A vessel used for decanting or receiving decanted liquors: *spec.* a bottle of clear flint or cut glass, with a stopper, in which wine is brought to the table, and from which the glasses are filled.
digester		A strong close vessel in which bones or other substances may be subjected to the action of water or other liquid at a temperature and pressure above those of the boiling point, so as to be dissolved. In its original form called from its inventor, *Papin's digester.*
dog-grate		A detached fire-grate standing in a fireplace upon supports called dogs. [AKA: andiron.]
dredger	drudger	[1. A box with a perforated lid for sprinkling powder over anything, as a flour-dredger. 2. A shaker of salt or sugar. Cited in Feild.]

Usage	Probable Source of Term and Cognates	Earliest Citation
		1846
		1715
		1681
		1881
		1666

Kitchen Utensils

Term	Variant Spellings	Definition
dripping pan		A pan used to catch the "dripping" from roasting meat.
estamin	estemina, stamina, estamene, etamine	An open woollen fabric, used for making sieves, etc. In 18th c. also applied to some silk fabric, presumably of similar texture.
ewer	ewere, euer, ewar, ewear, ewyr, hure, yore, eure, ower, ure, yower, ewre, eawer, eawr	"A pitcher with a wide spout, used to bring water for washing the hands." In [modern] use the trade name for a bedroom water-jug.
fat	faet, faett, fet, feat, fatte, fate, faat	A vessel of large size for liquids; a tub, a dyer's or brewer's vat, a wine cask. [A keeler.]
flagon	flagan, flakon, flacon(e), flaccoun, flackoun, flagone, flagon	1. A large bottle for holding wine or other liquors; in early use sometimes *spec.* a metal bottle with a screw top, such as was carried by pilgrims. 2. A large vessel containing a supply of drink for use at table; now *esp.* one with a handle and spout, and usually a lid.
flake	flek(e), fleyke, fleake, flaik, fleak, fleack, flake, fleigh, fleak	A [wooden] frame or rack for storing provisions, in [modern] use *esp.* oat-cakes [often suspended from the ceiling to keep from rats or mice.] [AKA: creel.]

Usage	Probable Source of Term and Cognates	Earliest Citation
		1463
	Fr., Sp., Pg., It.	1714
	AF., OF.	1325
Obs.	OE., MLG., Du., OHG., MHG., ON.	1225
	ME., OF.	1470–1485
	ON., Da., MDu., Du., MLG., Ger.	1420

Term	Variant Spellings	Definition
flask	flasce, flaxe, flaske, flasque	1. In [Old English], a vessel of wood, skin, or other material, for carrying liquor. 2. A bottle of glass or metal, somewhat flat in shape and of size suitable to be carried in the pocket, intended to contain a supply of wine or other beverage for use on a journey; usually furnished with a screw-top and (when made of glass) encased in leather for protection.
flasket	flaskett, flaskit	1. "A long shallow basket." 2. A similar article made of metal. 3. "A shallow washing tub." 4. A small flask.
fleeter		[Skimming spoon. Cited in Feild.]
flesh-hook		1. A hook to hang meat upon; a "pot-hook." 2. A hook for removing meat from the pot.
frying pan		A shallow pan, usually of iron, with a long handle, in which food is fried. [Often fitted on to an iron frame indenitical in shape to the pan's top rim. Easily swung into or out of fire. Hangs from a racheted hook which is attached to a crane or sway. Cited in Harrison.]

Usage	Probable Source of Term and Cognates	Earliest Citation
Obs.	Found in all Teutonic and Romance languages	900
	OF.	1460–1465
		1325, 1596

Term	Variant Spellings	Definition
funnel	fonel(le), funell, fonnell, funelle	A cone-shaped vessel usually fitted at the apex with a short tube, by means of which a liquid, powder, or the like, may be conducted through a small opening.
gallipot	galy pott, gale pote, galey potte, galeye pot, gallie potte, gally pot, gollee-pot, galley-pot, galipot	A small earthen glazed pot, *esp.* one used by apothecaries for ointments and medicines.
gimlet	gymlotte, gymley, gymlett, gymblett	A large shallow tub, used for salting bacon and for other purposes.
gipse		[A wooden spice or sugar mortar. Cited in Phipps.]
goffer	gauffer, gauffre	1. A goffering tool. 2. "An ornamental plaiting used for the frills and borders of women's caps."
goggan	goggon, goggen	A wooden or metal dish.
gourd		The "shell" or whole rind of the fruit dried and excavated, used as a water-bottle [or a ladle, dipper, scoop]. [AKA: calabashe.]
grater	grateor, gratour, gratoir, grattoir, gratoire	An instrument with a rough indented surface used for grating or rasping; *esp.* a kitchen utensil, having a rasping surface formed by punching holes which raise protuberances, and used for grating ginger, nutmegs, etc.

Usage	Probable Source of Term and Cognates	Earliest Citation
	ME., OF., Pr.	1402–1403
		1465
Obs.	OF., Fr.	1391
	Fr., AF., MLG.	1865
Dial.		1586
		1596
	OF.	1390–1391

Term	Variant Spellings	Definition
grinder		1. An instrument for grinding. 2. A muller or pestle.
harnen		[A free-standing wrought-iron toasting stand for drying out baked hearth-cakes. AKA: A cake stand. Cited in Feild.]
hook (huke obs. form)	hoc, hooc, hok, hoke, houk, howk, hooke, hooche, hwick	1. A length of metal, or piece of wood or other material, bent back, or fashioned with a sharp angle, often forming a part of something, as a pole, chain, etc., adapted for catching hold, dragging, sustaining suspended objects, or the like. (Frequently with a qualification indicating shape or use, as *chain-hook*, *chimney-hook*, *clip-hook*, *fire-hook*, *flesh-hook*, *gaff-hook*, *meat-hook*, *pot-hook*.)
huller		That which hulls; *spec.* a machine for separating the hulls from seeds.
infuser		1. One who infuses or pours in. 2. A vessel for making infusion [*esp.* with tea leaves].
iron crow		A bar of iron usually with one end slightly bent and sharpened to a beak, used as a lever or prise; a crow-bar.
jagger		That which jags; *spec.* a jagging-iron.

Usage	Probable Source of Term and Cognates	Earliest Citation
Obs.		1688
Obs.	OE., LG., MDu., MLG., Du., OHG., ON., Sw., Da.	900
		1864
		1899
		1400
		1864

Irish cake stool (a.k.a. harnen or griller). Niina Aaalto.

Kitchen Utensils

Term	Variant Spellings	Definition
jar	iarre, jarr	1. A vessel of earthenware, stoneware, or glass, without spout or handle (or having two handles), usually more or less cylindrical in form. [Originally] used only in its eastern sense of a large earthen vessel for holding water, oil, wine, etc. 2. A low glass vessel shaped like a gallipot.
jigger	gygger, giger, gigger	A drink of spirits, a dram. Also, a small glass or metal cup, a measure used in mixing cocktails; the contents of such a glass or measure.
keeler	kelare, kyler, kieler, kealer, keakor, keellar	A vessel for cooling liquids; a shallow tub used for household purposes.
kibble	keeble, kible	A large wooden or (later) iron bucket, for conveying ore or rubbish to the surface. [A wooden bucket used to draw water from the well. Cited in Phipps.]
kilp	kylpe, kelpe, kilpe, klip, kelp	The moveable or detachable handle (pair of clips) of a pot or cauldron; also, a pot-hook or crook from which a pot is suspended; the bail or hoop-handle of a pot or kettle; rarely a hook in general.
kimnel	kembelina, kymbelina, kemelyn, kemeline, kemeling, kymlen, kymlling, gimlen, kimline, kimlinge, kimblinge, kemelling,	A tub used for brewing, kneading, salting meat, and other household purposes.

Usage	Probable Source of Term and Cognates	Earliest Citation
	Fr., Pg., Sp., Pr., Arab.	1592, 1602
U.S.		1836
Obs.		1440
		1671
	NEng. dial., ON.	1425
Obs.	OE., ME.	1275

Term	Variant Spellings	Definition
	kimlin(g), gimlin, kymnell(e), kimenekk, kimnell, kimmell, kymnel, kimnel(l), kemell	
lade-	hladan, ladan, laden, lhade, lade, laid, hold, lode, laded, hladen, ladin, laden, ladyd, laded	[Combination form: lade-gorn = a pail with a long handle to lade water out with. Derb. Also called a lade-pail. Quoted by Halliwell.] [A wooden pail, of which one stave is longer and is used as a handle, for drawing water from a spring or larger vessel. Cited in Phipps.]
lamhog		[A wooden cup with solid handles. Cited in Phipps.]
laver	lavor, lavour(e), lavowre, lavre, lavyre, lawere, lower, lorre, levare, lavar, lawer, lawar(e), leyver	A vessel, basin, or cistern for washing; in early use, chiefly a wash-hand-basin or a water-jug, usually of metal; *occas.* a pan or bowl for water, irrespective of its purpose. Now only *poet,* or rhetorical.
limbeck	lambyke, lembike, -byke, lembyck, -beck, lymbeke, lim-, lymbeck(e), -bique, limbek, -bic(ke)	[A distilling apparatus]; an alembic.
loggerhead	loggerheat	An iron instrument with a long handle and a ball or bulb at the end used, when heated in the fire, for melting pitch and for heating liquids. [Often

Usage	Probable Source of Term and Cognates	Earliest Citation
	OE., ON.	1847
	OF.	1386
Obs.		1599
		1860

Term	Variant Spellings	Definition
		used to plunge into a flip (mixture of liquor)].
mier		[A horse-hair sieve. Cited in Feild.] [In England a sieve was made of horsehair, in U.S. made of wire.]
mill	mylen, myln, mulne, mylne, myllne, myllen, miln, myll, mulle, mille, mylle, melle, myl	A machine or apparatus for squeezing the liquid from fruit, vegetables, plants, by grinding or crushing [usually with defining prefix as cider mill.]
muffineer		1. A small castor with a perforated top for sprinkling salt or sugar on muffins. 2. A covered dish to keep toasted muffins [hot].
muller		A vessel in which wine [or other liquor] is mulled.
myour	miour(e), myoure, myowre, mture, myere	A [bread]-grater.
nappy	knappy, -nappey, napple	An earthenware or glass dish with sloping sides.
nappy cup		A bottle or cup to hold a drink of liquor.
nef	neff	A table ornament in the shape of a ship, usually made of intricately worked silver and originally used to hold condiments, table napkins, etc.

Usage	Probable Source of Term and Cognates	Earliest Citation
	MDu., Du., OHG., MHG., Ger., ON.	1676
		1806–1807
		1858
Obs.	OF.	1316–1317
	Obs. origin	1873
		1784
	Fr.	1567

Iron kettle with bail resting on rush mat. Mat prevents breaking kettle on hearthstone when removed hot from fireplace. At right wooden flesh hooks. Author photo.

113

Term	Variant Spellings	Definition
		[Generally in the shape of the hull of a ship, in which the napkins for the king's table are kept. Quoted by M. Edgeworth, 1834.]
pail	payle, paille, payelle, paile, pale	A vessel, usually of cylindrical or truncated obconical shape, made of wooden staves hooped with iron, or sheet-metal, etc., and provided with a bail or hooped handle; used for carrying milk, water, etc.
pancheon	panshin, panshion, panchion, panchin, panshon	A large shallow earthenware bowl or vessel, wider at the top than at the bottom, used for setting milk to stand in to let the cream separate, and for other purposes: sometimes applied to a bread-pan.
piggin	piggan, piggen, piggon, pigging, pickein	A small pail or cylindrical vessel, *esp.* a wooden one with one stave longer than the rest serving as a handle; a milking pail; a vessel to drink out of. Its size varies according to purpose: it is described as "holding near a pint," "containing about a quart," "holding from 1 to 2 gallons."
pitcher	picher, pycher, pychere, pychar, pychare, pitchaer, pitchard, pecher, pechir, pichier, picier, pechier, petier	A large vessel usually of earthenware, with a handle (or two ears) and usually a lip, for holding and pouring out liquids; a jug, a jug-shaped or vase-shaped vessel.

Usage	Probable Source of Term and Cognates	Earliest Citation
	OF.	1440
		1601
Dial.	Gael., LSc., Ir., W.	1554
	OF., ME., Fr., OHG.	1290

115

Term	Variant Spellings	Definition
pitter		A mechanical device for [removing] pits or stones from fruit.
platter	plater, platere, plaitter	A flat dish or plate for food; in later usage often a wooden plate.
porringer	porreger, porrager, porrynger, porrenger	A small basin or similar vessel of metal, earthenware, or wood, from which soup, broth, porridge, children's food, etc., is eaten: variously specialized in different localities. [AKA: Bleeding basins or tasters. Cited in Earle.]
posnet	postinet, possy, postenet, possenet, poscent, posnette, pos(s)enett, postnet, posnett, posnit, possnet, postnett	A small metal pot or vessel for boiling, having a handle and three feet. [AKA: A pipkin, a pot.]
pot	pott, potte, putte, poot, poyt, pat, patt	1. A vessel of cylindrical or other rounded form, and rather deep than broad, commonly made of earthenware or metal, used to hold various substances, liquid or solid, for domestic or other purposes. 2. Such a vessel used to contain wine, beer, or any other drink; either for drinking out of (as a pewter pot for beer, etc.), or for pouring the drink into smaller vessels (as a coffee-pot or teapot).
pot clips	pot hangers	A moveable handle of two parts for a pot, called clips. Also known as bouls,

Usage	Probable Source of Term and Cognates	Earliest Citation
U.S.		1884
Chiefly arch.	ME., AF.	1330
		1522
Arch. and dial.	ME., OF.	1327
	OE., ME., OFris., MDu., MLG., LG., ON.	1200
	Sc. & N. Eng.	1560

An iron posnet (a.k.a. pipkin or pot) with short iron handle. Could be set directly on coals of fireplace. Author photo.

Kitchen Utensils

Term	Variant Spellings	Definition
		bools. [Detachable pot handle, plain or adjustable hooks for suspending pots over a fire. Cited in Feild.]
print	priente, pryente, preynte, preent(e), prente, printe, prynte, preinte, preynt, prend	A pat of butter, moulded to a shape. [Usually from a butter mould.]
pudding-bag	pudding-poke	A bag in which a pudding is boiled.
ramekin	ramme(l)kin, ramequin, ramakin, ramaquin	A dish in which ramekins or other portions of food are baked and served. [Often a mould in which food was baked.]
reckon	racente, racete, rakente, rakende, raken, racon, rackan, recawnt, rekand, rekande, rekanth, rekenth, reckand, recken, recon, reckan	A chain or other apparatus by which cooking vessels are suspended over a fire; now usually a vertical bar pierced with holes, into one of which the pot-hook is inserted.
riddle	hriddel, riddil, riddill, riddell	A coarse-meshed sieve, used for separating chaff from corn, sand from gravel, ashes from cinders, etc.; the most usual form has a circular wooden rim with a bottom formed of strong wires crossing each other at right angles.
rolling-pin		A roller or cylinder of wood, glass, or other material, for rolling out dough or paste to the required thickness for pie-crusts, etc.

Usage	Probable Source of Term and Cognates	Earliest Citation
	ME., Du., Da., MLG., LG., OF.	1768
		1597
	Flem.	1706
Obs.	OE., ON., OHG., ME.	1400
	OE.	1100
		1589

119

Term	Variant Spellings	Definition
sad-iron		A smoothing iron, properly solid flat-iron, in contradistinction to a "box-iron." [In places known as a skillet.]
saddle quern		[The name of saddle-quern has been given to this form of grinding apparatus (a bed-stone slightly hollowed on its upper surface and a large oval pebble for a muller). Quoted in *OED* from *Anc. Stone Impl.* X. 226, J, Evans, 1872.] [The true saddle quern was a two-handed implement allowing only a to-and-fro movement of the upper stone. Quoted in *OED* from *Proc. Prehist. Soc.* IV.35.]
safe	save	A receptacle for the safe storage of articles: *esp.* A ventilated chest or cupboard for protecting provisions from insects and other noxious animals; a meat-safe.
saler	salure, salere, sallyer, seler	A salt-cellar.
salt-cellar	saler, sellere, seler, celler, seller, sellar, cellar	A small vessel used on the table for holding salt.
sanders	saunders, sandery	[An instrument to dress the same (*sc.* cold beef) called sanders. *New Syst. Cookery* 51] [Name given to a preparation of minced beef or other meat. *Encycl. Cookery (Garrett)* 11.377.]

Usage	Probable Source of Term and Cognates	Earliest Citation
		1761
		1867
		1440
Obs.	OF., Fr.	13..
		1434
		1827, 1892

Large stone quern with handle at rear of stone. Used to grind corn, wheat, rye, or oats. Author photo.

Kitchen Utensils

Term	Variant Spellings	Definition
scoop	scope, skowp, scowpe, skop(e), scoupe, skwpe, skupe, skoppe, scoope, skoope, scowp	A utensil for bailing out, ladling or skimming liquids; usually in the form of a ladle or a concave shovel with a straight handle.
scraper		An instrument for scraping with. [Combination forms:] *scraper-knife*, **scraper board** (used to scrap food particles from a cutting board). A bowl scraper.
scummer	scummar, schumour, scomeoure, skum(u)r, scomor, scommer, skumer, scomer, scowmar, scomur(e), scomour, scomowre, scommyr, schomore, scummour, scummowre, scwmure, skumoure, skomer, scommar, skomor, skwmmer, skommer, skummer, scumur, scumer	A shallow ladle or sieve for removing scum or floating matter from the surface of a liquid
sieve	sibi, sife, syfe, syfa, syfue, syffe, syff, siff, seyf, seyfe, sefe, seiffe, sive, siue, cive, syve, syue, cyve, scyve, seve, seue, sewe, ceve, seeue, ceeue, seeve, seave, scieve	1. A utensil consisting of a circular frame with a finely meshed or perforated bottom, used to separate the coarser from the finer particles of any loose material, or as a strainer for liquids. A sieve is usually distinguished from a *riddle* by having finer meshes. 2. Used as a measure, or for holding anything. Also, a kind of basket used chiefly for market produce. 3. [In U.S. early sieves were made from wire and in England from horse hair. Cited in Carlo.]

Usage	Probable Source of Term and Cognates	Earliest Citation
	MHG., MSw., MDu., Ger., WGmc., MLG., OTeut.	1330
Obs.		1387
	OE., MDu., MLG., OHG.	725

Term	Variant Spellings	Definition
sillabub, syllabub	solybubbe, sullabub, sullibib, sullibub, selybube, selibube, sellibub, sallibube, sillyebub, syllibub, sillie bube, cillibub, sillybob, sillabubbe	A glass, jug, pot.
skep	skip	A basket, hamper, [tub, etc., of locally varying size, form, and use]; the quantity of grain, malt, charcoal, etc., contained in [this].
skewer		A long wooden or metal pin, used especially to fasten meat or the like together, to keep it in form while being cooked. [AKA: larding needles. Cited in Feild.]
skimmer	skemour, skemere, skymour(e), skymere, skymer, skymmoure, skymber, schimmer	1. A shallow utensil, usually perforated, employed in skimming liquids; also, any utensil or implement by means of which skimming or some analogous process is performed. 2. In *U.S.* a clam or scallop, the shell of which may be used for skimming milk, etc. *Esp.* the black clam.
slice	sclyce, sclice, sclise, sclys(e), sclyise, sklyce, sklyse, sklysess, sklice, sklise, slyce, slyese, slise	1. A spatula used for stirring and mixing compounds. 2. One or other of several flattish utensils (sometimes perforated) used for various purposes in cookery, etc.
slicer	sclycer	An implement or instrument specially adapted or used for slicing.

Usage	Probable Source of Term and Cognates	Earliest Citation
		1677
	OE., ON., OHG.	
		1679
	OF.	1302, 1881
Obs.	OF.	1400, 1459
		1530

Term	Variant Spellings	Definition
spit box		A spittoon.
squeezer		A mechanical device or apparatus, an implement, by which pressure can be applied.
steel	steik	A cask of wine.
steelyard	stiliard, stilyard, stilliard, stilard, still-yard, steeleyard, steel-yard	A balance consisting of a lever with unequal arms, which moves on a fulcrum; the article to be weighed is suspended from the shorter arm, and a counterpoise is caused to slide upon the longer arm until equilibrium is produced [a notch indicates the weight].
sugar nippers		An implement for cutting loaf sugar into lumps. [AKA: sugar tongs.]
swig	swgg, swigge	[The Wassail Bowl or Swig, as it is termed at Jesus College in the University. Quoted in R. Cook in *Oxford Night Caps* 30.] [Combination form: swig-bowl, the large bowl—like a punch-bowl—in which swig is served. Quoted by G. F. Jackson *Shropsh. Word-bk.*]
swizzle-stick		A stick used for stirring drink into a froth. Also, a rod used to stir a mixed drink, or to flatten the effervescence of a cocktail.

Usage	Probable Source of Term and Cognates	Earliest Citation
Originally U.S.	Da., NFris.	1833
		1839
	Flem., LG.	1468
		1639
		1708, 1790
	Origin unknown	1827, 1832
		1879

Kitchen Utensils

Term	Variant Spellings	Definition
tazza	tazze	A shallow ornamental bowl or vase; properly, one supported on a foot.
tea-kettle		A kettle in which water is boiled for making tea.
temse	temes, temys, temeze, tymze, temze, tem(m)es, tempse, temize, tems, temmis, timse, teems	A sieve, *esp.* one used for bolting meal; a searce, a strainer. In [modern] local use *esp.* a sieve used in brewing.
thivel, thible	thyvelle, thyvil, thyvel, theevil, thieval, thibble, thybel, thavel, thaivel, thabble, theedle	A stick for stirring porridge or anything cooked in a pot; a potstick.
tiffany	tiffanie, tiffenay, tiffeney, tiffinie, tifine, tifnie, tiphany, tiffney	A kind of thin transparent silk; also a transparent gauze muslin, cobweb lawn. An article made of tiffany, as a head-dress, a garment, a sieve. [Flour separated from the bran by being worked through a hair-sieve tiffany, or temse. Quoted by J. Lewis in *Stud. Nidderdale*, 15.]
tinder-box		A box in which tinder was kept (also usually the flint and steel with which the spark was struck, and sometimes the brimstone matches with which the flame was raised).
toaster		[An instrument or] appliance [used] for toasting bread by the fire. [Combination forms:] toasting fork, **toaster-oven**.

Usage	Probable Source of Term and Cognates	Earliest Citation
		1824
		1705
Dial.	OE., MHG., LG., MDu., Du., EFris., NFris., HG.	1050
N. Dial.		1483
	OF.	1606, 1882
		1530
		1695

Term	Variant Spellings	Definition
toddy-stick	tarrie, tary, terry, taree, tarea, tadie, tadee, taddt, toddey, toddie	A spatula, usually of glass or metal, for stirring toddy; a beverage composed of whisky or other spirituous liquor with hot water and sugar. [Combination form:] **toddy-lifter**.
tongs	tang, tange, tangan, tangen, tangs, tangys, tangis, tang(g)es, tang(g)is, taingis, tayngis, tayngs, tangisis, tong, tonge, toenge, tongge, tongen, tunges, tongys, toonges, tongges, tonges, tonkes, thounges, tungs, tongues	An implement consisting of two limbs or "legs" connected by a hinge, pivot, or spring, by means of which their lower ends are brought together so as to grasp and take up objects which it is impossible or inconvenient to lift with the hand. [Combination forms:] smith's tongs, fire-tongs, sugar-tongs.
tray	trie, tri	A utensil of the form of a flat board with a raised rim, or of a shallow box without a lid, made of wood, metal, or other material, of various sizes and shapes (round, oval, etc.); now used for carrying plates, dishes, cups and other vessels, etc. [Combination forms:] *bread-tray, card-tray, tea-tray.*
trestle	trestele, trestell(e), trestiel, trestul, trestyll(e), trestil, trestyl, tresselle, trestell, trestal, tressel, tressle, traisle, threstle, traassel, trystell(e), trystel, tristell, tristil, trestill(e), tristle, trys(s)elle, trisselle, trostyle, trostell, trustyll, trussell, trussel, trusle, trussle, trustle	A support for something, consisting of a short horizontal beam or bar with diverging legs, usually two at each end; *esp.* one of a pair or set used to support a board so as to form a table. [Combination forms:] **trestle-table**, **trestle-board**.

Usage	Probable Source of Term and Cognates	Earliest Citation
	Hind.	1840
	OE., OLG., MDu., Du., OFris., OHG., MHG., ON., Da.	725
	OE., ON., OSw., OTeut.,	10..
	ME., OF., Fr.	13..

An iron toddy-stick. Niina Aalto.

Term	Variant Spellings	Definition
tun	tunne, toun, townne, toune, tunn, towne, tune, twn(e), tounne, tonne, tonn, tone, ton, toon	A large cask or barrel, usually for liquids, *esp*. wine, ale, or beer, or for various provisions. Less common than *cask*.
tureen	terrene, terene, terrine, tereen, turen(n)e, turenein, turrene	A deep earthenware or plated vessel (usually oval) with a lid, from which soup is served. Also a smaller vessel of similar shape for sauce or gravy.
turkey wing		[A wing feather of a turkey used to baste meat or baked goods with grease or butter. Also used to brush ashes from top of Dutch oven. Cited in Carlo.]
voider	woider, voyder, voyiar, vodyer, voydour, vydour, vodour, voidour	A receptacle into which something is voided or emptied: a tray, basket, or other vessel in which dirty dishes or utensils, fragments of broken food, etc., are placed in clearing the table or during a meal.
wafer-iron		An apparatus for baking wafers, consisting of two iron blades between which the paste is held. A thin crisp cake, baked between wafer-irons. [Combination forms:] **wafer-stamp, wafer tongs**.
water trough		[A watertight hollowed stone or wooden block used for boiling or stewing into which hot stones are

Usage	Probable Source of Term and Cognates	Earliest Citation
	OE., ME., OFris., OLG., LG., MDu., OHG., MHG., ON., MDu., Da., OF.	725
	OF.	1706
Obs. dia.	OF.	1466
		1834

(L to R.) A toaster or broiler, an engraved bedwarmer, a turner, a salamander or browning iron. Mercer Museum.

133

Term	Variant Spellings	Definition
		dropped to bring and keep water boiling. Cited in Phipps.]
whisk	quhisk, wysk, whysk, whiske, wiske, wisk	1. An instrument, now freq[uently] a bundle of wires for beating up eggs, cream, or the like. 2. A bundle or tuft of twigs, hair, feathers, etc. fixed on a handle, used for brushing or dusting; also a water-sprinkler.

Usage	Probable Source of Term and Cognates	Earliest Citation
	ON., Sw., Norw., OHG., MHG., MDu., LG.	1666, 1729

CUTLERY

Term	Variant Spellings	Definition
fork	forca, force, forcke, furken	An instrument with two, three, or four prongs, used for holding the food while it is being cut, for conveying it to the mouth, and for other purpose at table or in cooking.
knife	knives, cnif, knif, cnife, cniue, kniue, knijf, knyue, knyf, knyff(e), knufe, cniues, cninfes, cuiufen, kniues, knifes, knyys, knifs	A cutting instrument, consisting of a blade with a sharpened longitudinal edge fixed in a handle, either rigidly as in a *table-[knife]*, *carving-[knife]*, or with a joint as in a *pocket-[knife]* or *clasp-knife*. The blade is generally of steel, but sometimes of other material, as in silver fish- and fruit-knives, the (blunt-edged) paperknife of ivory, wood, etc. and the flint knives of early man.
ladle	hlaedel, ladele, ladel, laddi, ladill, ladyl, ladyll(e), ladell(e), ladil, ladul	A large spoon with a long handle and cup-shaped bowl, used chiefly for lading liquids.
marrow-spoon		A [compound] spoon for extracting the marrow from bones.

Usage	Probable Source of Term and Cognates	Earliest Citation
	OE.	1463
	LOE., Fris., MDu., MLG., Ger., LG., ON., Sw., Da., OTeut.	1100
	OE.	1000
		1693

Term	Variant Spellings	Definition
prong	prange, prannge, prang, pronge, prongue, prung	An instrument or implement with two, three, or more piercing points of tines; a forked instrument, a fork. In many specific uses, now chiefly *dial.*; *e.g.* a fork to eat with, a table-fork; a long-handled fork for kitchen use; a kind of fire-iron; a rural implement, a pitchfork, hay-fork, dung-fork, digging-fork.
skymoure	straynoure	A ladle. [Gader it to-gederys with a ladle or a **Skymoure**. Quoted in *Two Cookeruy bks. 17.*]
spattle	spatl, spadl, spaöl, spatel, spatell, spatill, spatylle, spatele, spatyll, spattyl, spatle, spotle, spittle, spotel, spotele, spotil, spotell, spotyl	A spatula.
spatula		A simple implement of wood, ivory, or metal, having a flat elongated form with various modifications of shape and size, used for a variety of purposes. For stirring mixtures (*esp.* of a medical nature), spreading ointments or plasters, etc.
spittle	spitel, sputel, spytelle, spytyll, spitil, spittell	A baking implement; a shovel or peel.
spoon	spon, spone, sponne, spoune, spoun, spown, spoone, spoyn, spoine, spooin, spyne, speaun, speun, speean	A utensil consisting essentially of a straight handle with an enlarged and hollowed end-piece (the bowl), used

Usage	Probable Source of Term and Cognates	Earliest Citation
	MLG.	1492
	OE., OHG., MHG.	1430
Rare or obs., dial.	OE., MHG., OFris.	1440
	Sp., It.	1525
Dial.	OE.	1838
	OE., OFris., WFris., EFris., NFris., MLG., LG., ON., Icel., Norw.,	

Wall rack of hand carved birch wooden spoons. Author photo.

Term	Variant Spellings	Definition
		for conveying soft food or liquid to the mouth, or employed in the culinary preparation or other handling of [food]. [Combination forms:] horn spoon, silver spoon, wooden spoon, dessert spoon, marrow-spoon, mustard-spoon, salt-spoon, soup-spoon, table-spoon, tea spoon.
spurtle	spurtill, spurtil, spurtel, spirtle, spurkle	A flat implement used for turning oatcakes, etc. A wooden stick for stirring porridge, etc.; a pot-stick or "thivel."

Usage	Probable Source of Term and Cognates	Earliest Citation
	MSw., Sw., Da., OHG., MHG., MDu.	
Obs.		1677

COOKING

Term	Variant Spellings	Definition
beetle	bietel, bitel, bytel, bytylle, betel, betylle, bittill, betel(e), betill, betyll, betle, beetel(le), boytle, beatle, bittle	An implement consisting of a heavy weight or "head," usually of wood, with a handle or stock, used for crushing, bruising, beating, flattening, or smoothing, in various domestic operations, and having various shapes according to the purpose for which it is used.
boat	bat, bot, boot, boote, bote, boate, botte, boitt, bottes, bate, bait, bayt, bat(t)is	A vessel or utensil resembling a boat in shape: A dish used to serve sauces, etc. in.
boiler		A vessel in which water or any liquid is boiled.
boultel	bultell(e)	A kind of cloth specially prepared for sifting; a sieve [or] bolter, [thus a] degree of fineness as determined by the fineness of the sieve.
break-staff	brake-staff, braeke, braak, breken	A baker's kneading-machine. [The dough] is deposited on a strong

Usage	Probable Source of Term and Cognates	Earliest Citation
	OE., OTeut., MHG.	c897
	OE.	1684
		1540
Obs.		1266
	MHG., ODu., Du.	1440, 1836

Term	Variant Spellings	Definition
		wooden platform or table, called a *break*, to be operated upon by the breaksman who seizes a strong lever called a break-staff, with which he presses down the dough. Quoted by P. Barlow in *Encycl. Metrop (1845)* VII, 801/2.
casserole		A kind of stew-pan. Now, a dish cooked and served in a casserole.
cauldron, caldron	caudroun, cauderoun, cawdroun, caudren, cawdrone, cawdrun, cudron, cawdren, cawderowne, cawdurne, cawtron, caudryn, calderon, caldrone, cawdron, caudron, cartherne, caldsron	A large kettle or boiler.
chafing-dish	chaffyndyche, chafindish, chaffendish, chafen-dish, chaffing-dish	A vessel to hold burning charcoal or other fuel, for heating anything placed upon it; a portable grate.
cleaver	clevere, clyuer, clever, cleever	An instrument for cleaving; a butcher's chopper for cutting up carcasses.
coffin	cofine, coffyne, cowyne, cofyn(e), cofynne, cophinne, cophyn(e), cophin(e), coffine, coffyng, coffen	A basket. A mould of paste for a pie; the crust of a pie.
craft	craeft, creaft, creaeft, creft, crafte, crafft, creft, craifft	[In the general sense of vessels of all kinds] for water carriage [*e.g.*, a carafe.]

Usage	Probable Source of Term and Cognates	Earliest Citation
	Fr., It., Sp.	1725
	AF., ME., ONF., OF.	1300
		1483
		1449
Obs.	ME., OF.	1430
	OE., OFris., MDu., Du., LG., OHG., MHG., ON.	1769

An array of wooden birch adult and children trenchers. Bottom shelf, carved wooden scoops/spoons, a piggin with ears; middle shelf extreme right, carved wooden losset/wooden tray. Author photo.

Term	Variant Spellings	Definition
creeper	creopere, creper(e), crepar	A small iron frying-pan with three legs [AKA: a spider].
cresset	crassete, crescette, cresette, cresete, cressetyt, cressette, cressett, cres(s)hette, cressit	A vessel of iron or the like, made to hold grease or oil, or an iron basket to hold pitched rope, wood, or coal, to be burned for light, usually mounted on the top of a pole or building, or suspended from a roof. Frequently as a historical word; in actual use applied to a fire-basket for giving light on a wharf.
crock	crocca, krocke, crocke, crokk(e), crok	An earthen pot, jar, or other vessel. A pot of iron or other metal.
extractor	extracter	An instrument for drawing or pulling out anything, [esp.] extracting honey from the combs.
flesh-hook		A hook for removing meat from the pot. A hook to hang meat upon; a "pot-hook."
frying-pan		A shallow pan, usually of iron, with a long handle, in which food is fried.
gallipot	galy pott, gale pote, galey potte, galeye pot, gallie pot, gally pot, gollee-pot, galley-pot, galipot	A small earthen glazed pot, esp. one used by apothecaries for ointments and medicines.
grater	gratour, gratere	An instrument with a rough indented surface used for grating or

Usage	Probable Source of Term and Cognates	Earliest Citation
U.S. localized		1880
	OF.	1370
	OE., Du.	1000
		1875
		1325, 1596
		1382
		1465
	OF.	1390–1391

Term	Variant Spellings	Definition
		rasping; *esp.* a kitchen utensil, having a rasping surface formed by punching holes which raise protuberances, and used grating ginger, nutmegs, etc.
griddle	gredil(e), gridele, gridil, grydel, gradel(le), gredyl(e), grydele, grydell, grydyl, gridel, griddyll	A circular iron plate upon which cakes are baked; also used for cooking grills, etc. [AKA: a gridiron, now obsolete. AKA: a gofer or waffle iron, rare.]
hippocras bag		A conical bag of cotton, linen, or flannel, used as a filter or strainer.
jet	jett, jut	A spout or nozzle for emitting water, gas, etc.
lead		A large pot, cauldron, or kettle; a large open vessel used in brewing and various other operations. (Originally, one made of lead, but early used without reference to the material.)
lug		The handle of a pitcher, etc. Also [technical] in various uses, denoting an appendage by which an object may be lifted or suspended. [Also] the side-wall (of a fire-place or other recess); a (chimney) corner.
masher		A machine, [vessel, or instrument] for mashing [malt,] fruit, vegetables, etc.

Usage	Probable Source of Term and Cognates	Earliest Citation
	OF.	1352
Obs.		1601
		1825
Only dial.	OE., OFris., Du., MLG., Sw., Da., MHG.	1100
		1624, 1784
		1878

Term	Variant Spellings	Definition
monteith	monteigh, monteth, monteff, montait, monteph, montiff	A deep, ornamental, usually silver bowl having a scalloped rim from which drinking vessels may be hung, formerly used for cooling glasses or as a punch bowl.
mortar	mortere, morter, mortyer, moorter, morteer, mortier, mortre, mortore, morture, mortare	A [vessel] of a hard material (*e.g.* marble, brass, wood, or glass), having a cup-shaped cavity, in which ingredients used in pharmacy, cookery, etc., are pounded with a pestle.
mould	muld(e), molde, mowlid(e), moold(e), mowld(e), moulde, moald(e)	A hollow vessel, often of decorative shape, in which a mixture is made or left to set, so as to assume the same shape. Also, a pudding, etc., made in such a vessel.
nipper	nypper, knipper	[An instrument, usually made of iron or steel, having two jaws by which a thing may be firmly seized and held, or cut through, by pressure exerted upon the handles; forceps, pincers, pliers. Usually to nip off a piece of sugar from a block of sugar. Cited in Feild.]
pan	panne, ponne, pon, pane	A vessel, of metal or earthenware, for domestic uses, usually broad and shallow, and often open.

Usage	Probable Source of Term and Cognates	Earliest Citation
Hist.		1683
	OE., MLG., OHG., MHG., Ger., OSw., Sw., Da.	1000
U.S. "mold"	ME., OF.	1573
	OE., OLG., OFris., MLG., LG., MDu., Du., OHG., MHG., Icel., Sw., Da.	897

Wooden mortar approx. 28 inches in height with carved wooden beater/pestle. Author photo.

Term	Variant Spellings	Definition
pattypan	pateepan, pattipan, pattepan	A pasty [pastry] baked in a small pan. A small tin pan or shape in which patties are baked.
peel	pele, peele, piele, peale, pale	A shovel or shovel-shaped implement: now locally or dialectally applied to a fire-shovel, and in some technical uses. A baker's shovel, a pole with a broad flat disk at the end for thrusting loaves, pies, etc., into the oven and withdrawing them from it. [AKA: a slice.]
pewterwort		A name given to the plant *Equisetum hyemale* on account of its use in polishing pewter and other utensils.
pipkin	pypkin, pipken	A small earthenware pot or pan, used chiefly in cookery. In U.S. a small wooden tub having a vertical handle formed by the prolongation of one of the staves, a piggin.
poacher		A vessel or pan for poaching eggs, usually with shallow cup-like compartments in which an egg can be cooked over boiling water. Also, a vessel or pan in which fish, etc. can be poached.
pot	pott, potte, putte, poot, poyt, pat, patt	A vessel of cylindrical or other rounded form, and rather deep than broad,

Usage	Probable Source of Term and Cognates	Earliest Citation
		1694, 1710
	ME., OF., Fr.	1400
		1597
Dial. only in England		1565
		1861
Dial.	LOE., EME., OFris., MDu., Du., MLG., LG., LON., Sw., Da.	

Term	Variant Spellings	Definition
		commonly made of earthenware or metal, used to hold various substances, liquid or solid, for domestic or other purposes. Used for cooking or boiling. [Combination forms:] pot crook = pot hook.
powdering-tub		A tub in which the flesh of animals is "powdered," or salted and pickled.
quern	cweorn, coern, cern, cweorne, queern(e), quyerne, qwher, querne, queren, qwern, quearn, wherne, wyrne, queirn, quarn, quirn	A simple apparatus for grinding corn, usually consisting of two circular stones, the upper of which is turned by hand; also, a small hand-mill for grinding pepper, mustard, or similar substances. [Combination forms:] saddle quern, hand quern, hour glass quern.
roller	rollar, rouler, rouller, rowler, rowlar, rower, rouer, roler	A rolling-pin.
rower		[Large wooden paddles used to stir barley when brewing. Cited in Harrison.]
runge	runze	A kind of tub; [similar to a] ringe or flasket.
salamander	salamandre	A circular iron plate which is heated and placed over a pudding or other dish to brown it.

Usage	Probable Source of Term and Cognates	Earliest Citation
		1530
	OE., OFris., MDu., Du., OHG., MHG., ON., Sw., Da., Goth.	c990
Dial.		1420
Dial.		1574
	Fr., MHG., Ger.	1755

An unusual early iron skillet with small handles on opposite side. Author photo.

Kitchen Utensils

Term	Variant Spellings	Definition
scummer	scummar, schumour, scomeoure, skumo(u)r, scommer, skumer, scomer, scowmar, scomur(e), scomour, scomowre, scommyr, schomore, scummour, scummowre, scwmure, skumoure, skomer, scommar, skomor, skwmmer, skommer, skummer, scumur, scumer	A shallow ladle or sieve for removing scum or floating matter from the surface of a liquid. [AKA: a fleeter.]
sifter		A utensil or apparatus for sifting; a sieve; also *dial.*, a fire-shovel, kitchen shovel.
skep	sceppe, scep, scepp, scappe, scape, skeppe, skepp, skape, skeb, skepe, skeipp, scepe, skippe, skyppe, skype, skip, skib	A basket or hamper, varying in form and use in different localities. In local use, a coal-scuttle.
skillet	skelet, skellet, scellet	A cooking utensil of brass, copper, or other metal, usually having three or four feet and a long handle, used for boiling liquids, stewing meat, etc.; a saucepan, stew-pan.
slice	sclyce, sclice, sclise, sclys(e), sclyise, sklyce, sklyse, sklyss, sklice, sklise, slyce, slyese, slise	A spatula used for stirring and mixing compounds. [AKA: a peel.]
spattle	spatule	A spatula. [With a wooden spatle or spoone, beat them well together. Quoted in Plat. Jewell-ho II.38 in *OED*.]

Usage	Probable Source of Term and Cognates	Earliest Citation
Obs.	OF., Fr.	1326
		1611
	ON., Sw., Da., MHG., MDu., Du., OHG.	1300
Chiefly North America, a frying pan, a heavy cooking pan.		1403
Obs.	OF., Fr.	1400
Rare or obs.	LME.	1594

Large iron crane from which is suspended ratchycroke trammels, cast-iron kettle and hanging griddle, turner, spatula, ash shovel, cast-iron, baking iron, large cast-iron spit andirons, smaller andirons, various skimmers and ladles, leaning against fireplace wall, two fire pokers, fireplace tong. Mercer Museum.

Three long-handled skillets with legs. Could be placed directly over fire or coals. Mercer Museum.

Term	Variant Spellings	Definition
spider	spidra, spidre, spidere, spither, spyther, spyder, spidar	A kind of frying-pan having legs and a long handle; also loosely, a frying-pan. A trivet or tripod, griddle. [AKA: a creeper.]
spittle	spitel, sputel, spytelle, spytylle, spitil, spittell	A baking implement; a shovel or peel.
spurtle	spurtill, spurtil, spurtel, spirtle, spurkle	A flat implement used for turning oatcakes, etc. A wooden stick for stirring porridge, etc.; a potstick or "thivel."
strainer	streignour, streyngoure, streyour, streinor, stryn(n)or, streynour(e), straynour(e), strenour, straynowr(e), straywoure, streneyour, sterner, strenyor, strenyowre, streneyour, strynour, streyner, streyyoure, streynyowr, straygner, strenear, strenere, strenyer, streiner, strayner	A utensil or device for straining, filtering, or sifting; a filter, sieve, screen, or the like.
tammy		A strainer. [To] strain or rub through a tammy [cloth] into another clean stewpan [as in straining fruit or vegetables]. A fine sieve. [To squeeze juice from berries and grapes.]
thivel, thible	thyvelle, thyvil, thyvel, theevil, thieval, thibblele, thybel, thavel, thaivel, thabble	A stick for stirring porridge or anything cooled in a pot; a pot stick.

Usage	Probable Source of Term and Cognates	Earliest Citation
Originally U.S.	OE.	1807
	OE.	1876
Obs.		15..
		1326–1327
		1769
		1483

Hanging Betty lamp. Mercer Museum.

Term	Variant Spellings	Definition
timbale		[Combination form]: timbale-iron, a cooking utensil with a bulging head used to form a cup-shaped crust.
trap	treppe, traeppe, trapp, trappe	A kind of dish or pan, for baking. [A baking tin for tarts.]
tunnel	tonel, tonell, tonnel, tonnell, tunell, tunill	A funnel.
turnel		A tub; *esp.* a shallow oval tub.
urn	wrn, vrne, uryn, urne	An earthenware or metal vessel or vase of a rounded or ovaloid form and with a circular base, used by various peoples *esp.* in former times to preserve the ashes of the dead. [Now] an oviform pitcher or vessel for holding water, etc.; a water-pitcher, water-pot.
vessel	vessele, wessele, vesselle, wesselle, vessale, vescel, vessil, wessel, uessel, fessel, wessell, fessell, vesseal, veseal, vessall, vyscele, weschele, wesch, veschale, wes(s)chael(le), wischeall, veschall, weschall, vesscheall, weschail, veschell, vesschell, veshel, veshell, vessayle, veassayle, vessaile, vayssel	Any article designed to serve as a receptacle for a liquid or other substance, usually one of circular section and made of some durable material; *esp.* a utensil of this nature in domestic use, employed in connexion with the preparation or serving of food or drink and usually of a size suitable for carrying by hand. [Many combination forms]: milk vessel, wine-vessel, drinking vessel.

Usage	Probable Source of Term and Cognates	Earliest Citation
		1895
Obs.	ME., MDu., WFlem., OF.	1390
Obs.	OF.	1529
Obs.		1688
	It., Sp., Pg., Fr.	1374
	AF., OF., Fr., Pg., Sp., It.	1300

Kitchen Utensils

Term	Variant Spellings	Definition
yetling	yet(t)lying, yettlyne, yetteling, yetlyn(g), yetline, yaitling, yetlen, yetatelin, yet(t)lin, yetland, yetlan, yettling	A pot or boiler, usually of cast iron; *esp.* one with a bow-handle and three feet. [AKA: a "girdle" (gridiron) on which cakes are baked. A Dutch oven only in America.]

Usage	Probable Source of Term and Cognates	Earliest Citation
		1378–1379, 1566

Appendix

In the utensils table a total of of 383 items are identified of which 196 are of a known etymological source and 187 items are unknown. Thirty-one of the identified items are of a dialect that still may or may not be in active usage.

Sixty-eight identified names of items are obsolete and 12 are archaic. Three hundred five identified utensil names remain in use.

Notes

Introduction

1. Francis Phipps, *Colonial Kitchens, Their Furnishings, and their Gardens* (NY: Hawthorn Books, Inc., 1972); Joyce W. Carlo, *Trammels, Trenchers, and Tarlets* (Old Saybrook, CT: Peregrine Press, 1982).

Coming to the New World

1. Noah Webster, *American Spelling Book* (Wilmington, Delware: Bonsal and Niles, 1802).
2. Noah Webster, *An American Dictionary of the English Language* (New Haven, CT: Hezekiah Howe, 1828).
3. Jeremy Smith, *An Historical Study of English: Function, Form, and Change* (London: Routledge, 1996).
4. Ibid.
5. Albert C. Baugh and Thomas Cable, *A History of the English Language, 3 rd ed.* (London: Routledge & Kegan, 1978).
6. Ibid.
7. Iassc Candler quoted in Baugh, *A History of the English Language.*
8. Richard Bailey, *Pilgrim Possessions as Told by Their Wills and Inventories* (Deerfield, MA: Henry N. Flynt Library, 1951).
9. "Mourt, G." *Mourt's Relation: A Relation or Journal of the Proceedings of the Plantation Settled at Plymouth in New England. Nov.1620 to Oct. 1621.* (Regarded as a collaboration of William Bradford and Edward Winslow.) Available online at: http://members.aol.com/calebj/mourt.html, last accessed 11 March 2002.
10. John W. Oliver, *History of American Technology* (NY: Ronald Press Co., 1975).
11. Frances Phipps, *Colonial Kitchens, Their Furnishings, and their Gardens* (NY: Hawthorn Books, Inc., 1972).
12. Ibid.
13. Bernard Bailyn, *Voyagers to the West A Passage in the Peopling of America on the Eve of the Revolution* (NY: Vintage, 1986).
14. Adolph B. Benson, ed., *Peter Kalm's Travels in North America: The English Version of 1770* (NY: Dover Pub. Inc., 1964).
15. Ibid.
16. Ibid.
17. Ibid.
18. Rachel Feild, *Irons in the Fire: A History of Cooking Equipment* (Ramsbury, Marlborough, UK: The Crowood Press, 1984).

Bibliography

American Hearth, The. Monograph. Binghamton, NY: Broome Historical Society, Cojac Printing Corp, 1976. A catalogue with excellent photographs of utensils accompanied by brief descriptions. Good source for information on the measurements of utensils.

Bailey, Richard. *Pilgrim Possessions as Told by Their Wills and Inventories*. Deerfield, MA: Henry N. Flynt Library, 1951. An indispensable listing of the contents of wills and inventories of estates as pertains to the fireplace and cooking utensils in the early colonial period.

Bailyn, Bernard. *Voyagers to the West: A Passage in the Peopling of America on the Eve of the Revolution*. NY: Vintage. 1986. This volume remains the definitive study of migration patterns from England and Scotland between 1773 and 1776. It includes charts, graphs, maps, detailed gender and age of immigrants, occupations, home residences and more of the over 9,300 immigrants between 1773 and 1776 that immigrated.

——. *North America: An Introduction* NY: Knopf, 1986. A series of lectures that offer four propositions of why and how the Colonies attracted the people of England, Scotland and Europe.

Baugh, Albert C. and Thomas Cable. *A History of the English Language*. 3rd. ed. London: Routledge & Kegan, 1978. An excellent text updated with new studies of the development of the English language.

Bridenbaugh, Carl. *The Colonial Craftsman*. Chicago: University of Chicago Press, 1964. Treatment of the colonial craftsman, his craft, and working conditions. Discusses in depth the need of Colonial America for craftsmen and the setting up of early factories such as for the production of church bells, glass making, textiles, and iron foundries.

Carlo, Joyce W. *Trammels, Trenchers, and Tarlets*. Old Saybrook, CT: Peregrine Press, 1982. Focuses primarily on New England historic houses, dining customs, the fireplace, and detailed recipes of early dishes. Photographs of fireplaces and some utensils.

Davidson, Marshall B. *Our Medieval Heritage*. NY: American Heritage Publishing Company, 1967. A general treatment of the lifestyle of the American colonists of the seventeenth century. Comments on their tools, household goods, crafts, and early industries.

Earle, Alice Morse. *Home Life in Colonial Days*. NY: Macmillan Company, 1945. An overview of life in colonial America focusing on the fireside, the serving of meals, kinds of food and drink, and neighborly friendliness. Tends to romanticize life of the times but does record many interesting anecdotes.

Ekkirch, A. Roger. *Bound for America: The Transportation of British Convicts to the Colonies, 1718–1775*. Oxford: Clarendon Press, 1987. A massive study of the transportation of over

Bibliography

30,000 British convicts to the Colonies. Graphs, detailed notes, political rationales, and punishments of the period in England.

Feild, Rachel. *Irons in the Fire: A History of Cooking Equipment.* Ramsbury, Marlborough, UK: The Crowood Press, 1984. The author offers a good history of cooking utensils, the dating of utensils, recipes, influences, and word origins. Deals mainly with English utensils and kitchens. Good photographs.

Harrison, Molly. *The Kitchen in History.* Reading, Berkshire, UK: Osprey Publishers, Ltd., 1972. A very readable history of the kitchen from pre-history to the twentieth century. Sees the kitchen as a center of influence. Many anecdotes about words, customs, and the hardships of the life of cook. Good illustrations.

Noel-Hume, Ivor. *A Guide to Artifacts of Colonial America.* NY: Knopf, 1976. An interesting and readable narrative of artifacts unearthed at Williamsburg, Virginia. Excellent examples on the dating of items and the process of establishing provenance of the artifacts.

Nutting, Wallace. *Furniture Treasury (Mostly of American Origin) All Periods of American Furniture with Some Foreign Examples in America Also American Hardware and Household Utensils, Five Thousand Illustrations with Descriptions on the Same Page. Volumes I and II in one.* Unabridged. New York: Macmillan Publishing Company, Inc., 1928. This work was originally published in two volumes in 1924, without page numbers. A republication, unabridged and unaltered, was published in 1965 in two volumes by Dover Publishing, Inc., New York in a slightly reduced size. This is an excellent source for photographs with an informal running commentary. Has become a standard for researchers and antique dealers.

Oliver, John W. *History of American Technology.* NY: Ronald Press Company, 1975. A broad overview of the developing crafts and manufacturing industries in America. Discusses science, transportation, and technologies such as clothing, buildings, agriculture,and small industries in the colonial period. Brief as it is, the factual data and notes make for a worthwhile read.

Peter Kalm's Travels in North America: The English Version of 1770. Adolph B. Benson, ed. NY: Dover Publishers, Inc., 1964. This work is a seminal volume of the colonial period with Kalm's acute observations of lifestyles, soil conditions, agricultural methods, Indians, types of homes built, and their furnishings. Kalm's travels were from the Middle Colonies to the Southern colonies back up through western Pennsylvania and into Canada. An essential read for anyone attempting to "see" the colonies in 1770.

Phipps, Frances. *Colonial Kitchens, Their Furnishings, and their Gardens.* NY: Hawthorn Books, Inc., 1972. A very readable and detailed study of kitchens and kitchen equipment in America from Jamestown, Virginia, to the eighteenth century. Very excellent photographs of most utensils plus an extensive bibliography.

Smith, Jeremy. *An Historical Study of English: Function, Form and Change.* London: Routledge, 1996. This lucid history of the evolution of the English language includes the great vowel shift, and linguistic terms. It describes how language functions and provides an excellent overview of the processes of change in a language.

Taylor, Dale. *Everyday Life in Colonial America.* Cincinnati, OH: Writer's Digest Books, 1997.

Bibliography

A specific and detailed history of the dating of the four regional colonies: New England, the Middle Colonies, and the Chesapeake area, and the Deep South. Includes discussion on the origins of immigrants, lifestyles, laws, customs, etc.. A guide for writers of the colonial period. Good bibliography.

Additional Sources

Barlow, Ronald S. *A Price Guide to Victorian Houseware: Hardware & Kitchenware*. El Cajon, CA: Windmill Publishing Company, 1992.

Bishop, Christina. *Miller's Collecting Kitchenware*. London: Reed Books, 1995.

Black, Maggie. *Food and Cooking in 19th Century Britain: History and Recipes*. Birmingham, England: English Heritage; Historic Buildings & Monuments Commission for England, 1985.

——. *A Taste of History: 10,000 Years of Food in Britain*. London: English Heritage in Association with British Museum Press, 1994.

Brooks, Sheena. *Hearth & Home: A Short History of Domestic Equipment*. London: Mills & Boon Ltd., 1973.

Creznic, Jean. "Old Kitchen Stuff," *Early American Homes* 29, 1 (Feb. 1998): 45–43.

Deetz, James. *In Small Things Forgotten: The Archaeology of Early American Life*. NY: Anchor, 1997.

Ettlinger, Steve. *The Kitchenware Book*. NY: Macmillan Co., 1992.

Evan-Thomas, Owen. *Domestic Utensils of Wood: XVIth to XIXth Century: A Short History of Wooden Articles in Domestic Use from the Sixteenth to the Middle of the Nineteenth Century*. London: Owen Evan-Thomas Ltd., 1932.

Eveleigh, David J. *Old Cooking Utensils*. Aylesbury, Bucks, UK: Shire Publishers, Ltd., 1986.

Felt, Joseph B. *The Customs of New England*. NY: Burt Franklin, 1970.

Franklin, Linda Campbell. *300 Years of Kitchen Collectibles*. AL: Books Americana Inc., 1991.

Gould, Mary Earle. *Early American Wooden Ware*. Rutland, VT: Charles E. Tuttle Company, 1962.

Hieatt, Constance and Sharon Butler. *Cuyre on Inglysh: English Culinary Manuscripts of the Fourteenth Century (Including the Forme of Cury)*. The Early English Text Society, Oxford, UK: Oxford University Press, 1985.

Jones, Maldwyn Allen. *American Immigration*. Chicago: University of Chicago Press, 1960.

Jordon, Terry G. and Matti Kaups. *The American Backwoods Frontier*. Baltimore: Johns Hopkins University Press, 1989.

Kauffman, Henry J. *The American Fireplace: Chimneys, Mantlepieces, Fireplaces & Accessories*. NY: Gallahad Books, 1972.

Kiell, Norman. *Food and Drink in Literature: A Selectively Annotated Bibliography*. Lanham, MD: Scarecrow Press, Inc., 1995.

Kraus, Michael. *Immigration, The American Mosaic: From Pilgrim to Modern Refugee*. Huntington, NY: Krieger Publisher Company, 1979.

Lifshey, Earl. *The Housewares Story: A History of the American Housewares Industry*. Chicago: National Housewares Manufactures Association, 1973.

Marshall, Jo. *Kitchenware*. Radnor, PA: Chilton Book Company, 1976.

Martyn, Charles. *Foods and Culinary Utensils of the Ancients*. NY: Caterer Publishing Company, nd.

McNerney, Kathryn. *Kitchen Antiques: 1790–1940*. Paducah, KY: Collector Books, 1993.

"Mourt, G." *Mourt's Relation: A Relation or Journal of the Proceedings of the Plantation Settled at Plymouth in New England. Nov. 1620 to Oct. 1621*. Regarded as a collaboration of William Bradford and Edward Winslow. http://members.aol.com/calebj/mourt. html, 11 March 2002.

Norwak, Mary. *Kitchen Antiques*. NY: Praeger Publishers, 1975.

Oxford Symposium on Food and Cookery 1988. Tom Janie, ed. London: Prospect Books Ltd., 1989.

Serjeantson, M. S. "The Vocabulary of Cookery in the Fifteenth Century," *Essays and Studies by Members of the English Association* XXIII. Collected by S. C. Roberts. Oxford: Clarendon Press, 1938.

Sim, Alison. *The Tudor Housewife*. Montreal: McGill-Queens's University Press, 1996.

Sinclair, Charles G. *International Dictionary of Food & Cookery*. Chicago: Fitzroy Dearborn Publishers, 1998.

Smith, David G and Charles Wafford. *The Book of Griswold & Wagner with Price Guide*. Atglen, PA: Schiffer Publishing Company, 1995.

Turgeon, Laurier. "The Tale of the Kettle: Odyssey of an Intercultural Object," *Ethnohistory: Bulletin of the Ohio Valley Historic Indian Conferenc* 44, I (Winter 1997): 1–29.

Warren, Geoffrey. *Kitchen Bygones: A Collector's Guide*. London: Souvenir Press Ltd., 1984.

Webster, Noah. *American Spelling Book*. Hartford, CT.: Hudson and Goodwin, 1783.

Willison, George F. *Saints & Strangers*. NY: Reynal and Hitchcock, 1945.

Internet site

http://www.ansteorra.org/mailman/listinfo/sca-cooks

Dictionaries

Concise Scots Dictionary, The. Mairi Robinson, ed. Aberdeen, Scotland: Aberdeen University Press, 1985.

Dictionary of Obsolete and Provincial English. Thomas Wright, complier. London: Henry G. Bohn, 1857. Republished by Gale Research Co. Detroit: Book Tower, 1967.

Dwelly's Illustrated Gaelic–English Dictionary. 9th ed. Edward Dwelly, complier. Glasgow: Gairm Publishers., 1977.

English Dialect Dictionary, The. Vol. 1, Joseph Wright, ed. Oxford: Oxford University Press, 1923.

Johnson, Samuel. *A Dictionary of the English Language*. Facsimile, 4th ed. London: Times Books, 1979.

Oxford English Dictionary. 1st, 2nd, eds. Oxford University Press, 1888, 1989. (See http://dictionary. oed.com/entrance.dtl (available through paid subscription only) for *3rd* ed. in progress, March 2002.)

Ray, John. *Dictionariolum Trilingue, Edito Prima, 1675*. Facsimile with an Introduction by

Bibliography

William Stearn. London: The Ray Society, 1981.

Webster, Noah. *An American Dictionary of the English Language. 2 vols.* New Haven, CT.: Hezekiah Howe, 1828.

Zupko, Ronald Edward. *A Dictionary of English Weights and Measures from Anglo-Saxon Times to the Nineteenth Century.* Madison, Wisconsin: University of Wisconsin Press, 1969. A comprehensive compilation of weights and measures with indicated origins, spellings, and use whether for dry or liquid contents. Arranged alphabetically.

Index

Index